LOCKE & KEY

WELCOME TO LOVECRAFT

WRITTEN BY

JOE HILL

ART BY

GABRIEL RODRIGUEZ

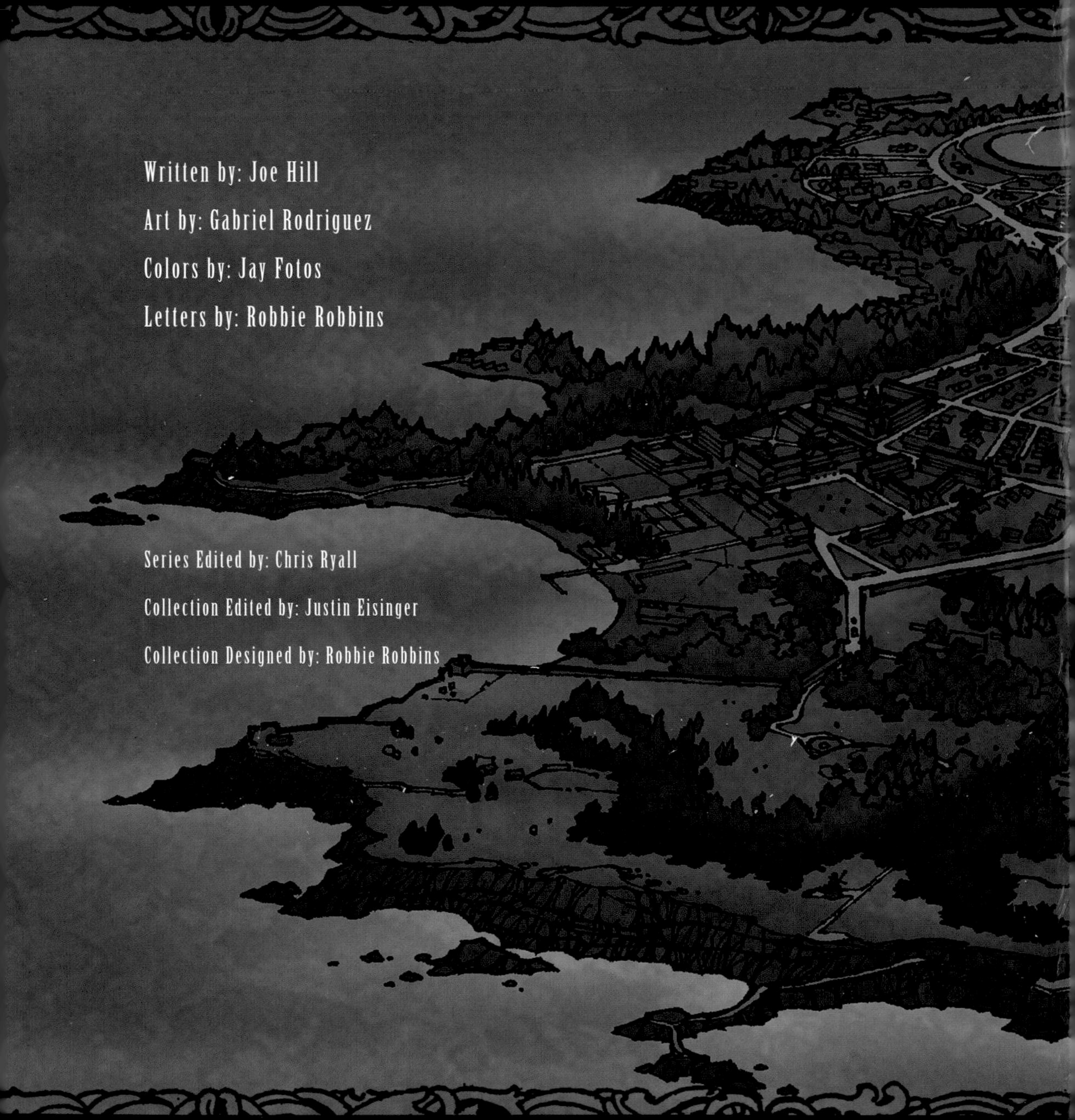

Written by: Joe Hill

Art by: Gabriel Rodriguez

Colors by: Jay Fotos

Letters by: Robbie Robbins

Series Edited by: Chris Ryall

Collection Edited by: Justin Eisinger

Collection Designed by: Robbie Robbins

Locke & Key created by Joe Hill and Gabriel Rodriguez

IDW founded by Ted Adams, Alex Garner, Kris Oprisko, and Robbie Robbins

ISBN: 978-1-60010-237-0

20 19 18 17 8 9 10 11

IDW

Ted Adams, CEO & Publisher
Greg Goldstein, President & COO
Robbie Robbins, EVP/Sr. Graphic Artist
Chris Ryall, Chief Creative Officer/Editor-in-Chief
Matthew Ruzicka, CPA, Chief Financial Officer
Alan Payne, VP of Sales
Dirk Wood, VP of Marketing
Lorelei Bunjes, VP of Digital Services

Become our fan on Facebook **facebook.com/idwpublishing**
Follow us on Twitter **@idwpublishing**
Check us out on YouTube **youtube.com/idwpublishing**
www.IDWPUBLISHING.com

Originally published as LOCKE & KEY: WELCOME TO LOVECRAFT Issues #1–6.

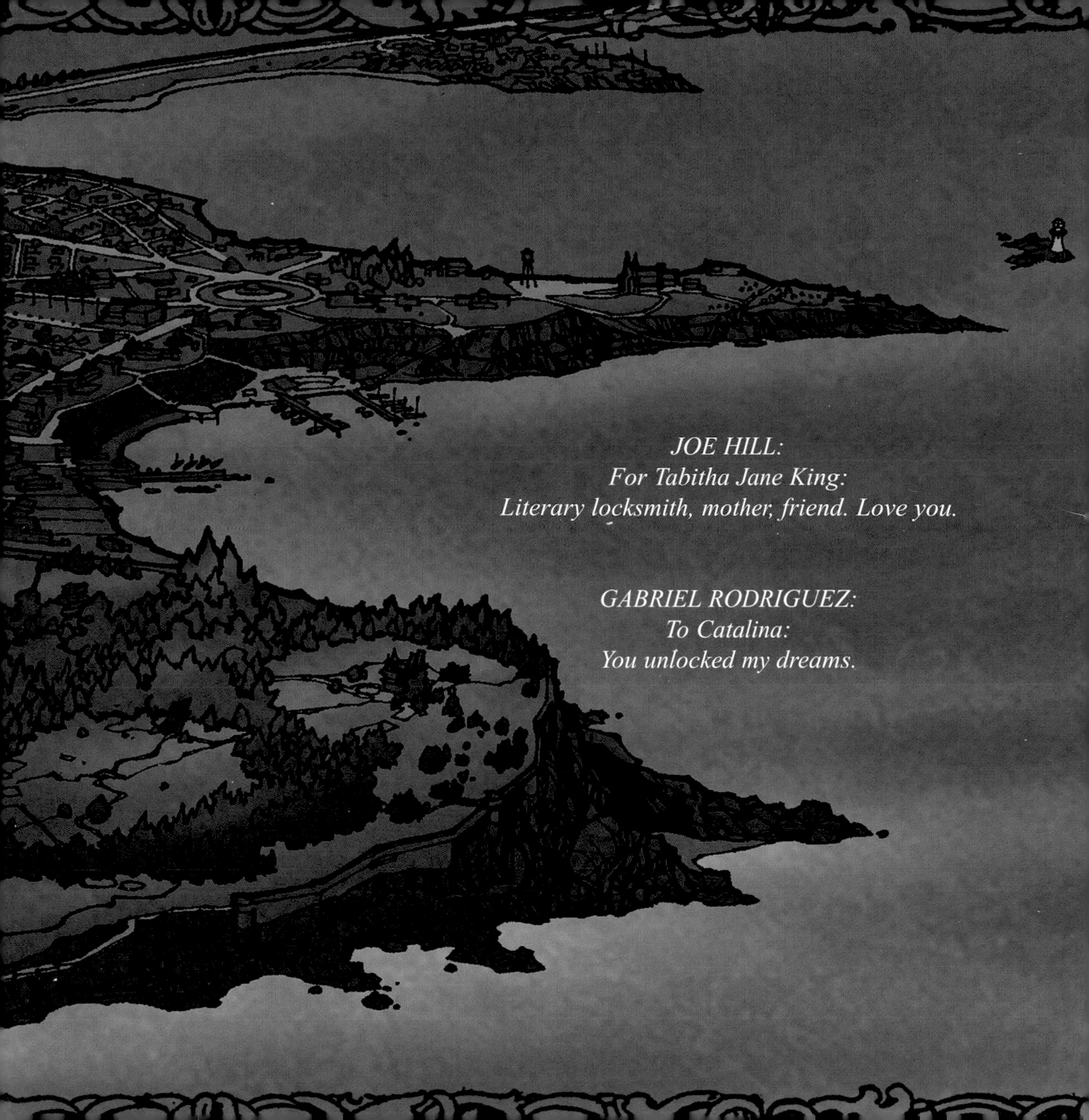

JOE HILL:
For Tabitha Jane King:
Literary locksmith, mother, friend. Love you.

GABRIEL RODRIGUEZ:
To Catalina:
You unlocked my dreams.

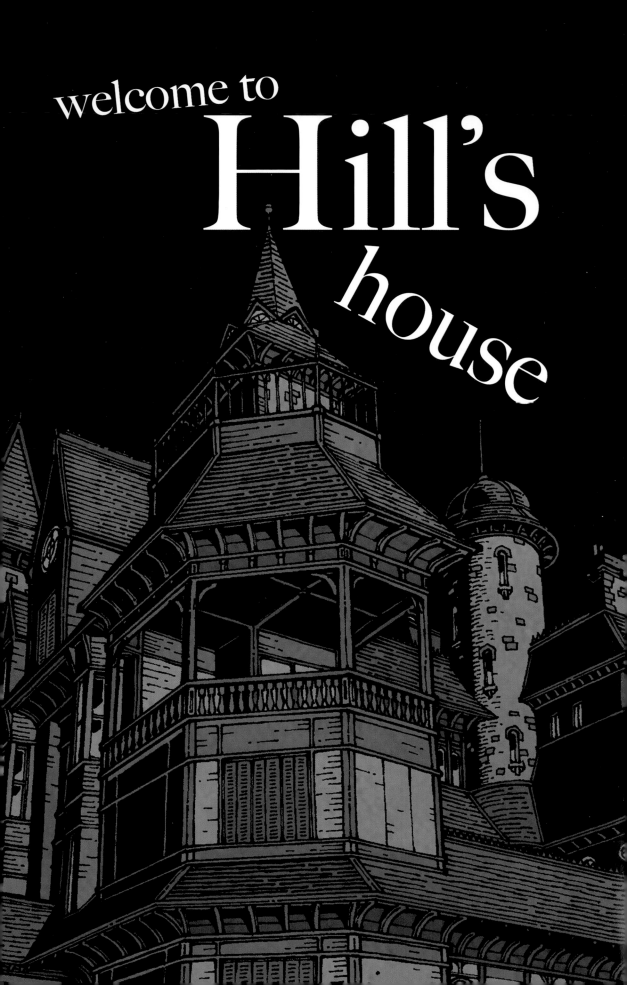

welcome to Hill's house

I was in London to promote a book called *The Watchman*, slamming between BBC radio interviews and bookstore stock signings when my UK publicist says, "We have another American writer in town. Shall we join up for lunch?"

So the two American writers got together, hunkering down over fish and potatoes in a hip little London restaurant not far from Trafalgar. The other guy was a tall, friendly dude with a thick beard, black duster, and easy smile–Joe Hill.

After swapping a couple of obligatory "touring writer" stories as we got to know each other, we discovered a mutual passion: Baseball. Being from Los Angeles, I bleed Dodger blue. Joe, from New England, is a hardcore member of Red Sox Nation. This was a perfect conversational match because so many ex-Dodgers were then playing for Boston (Julio Lugo and J.D. Drew among them, both of whom would bat over .330 in the upcoming post-season), and ex-BoSox were taking the field in Chavez Ravine (ace starting pitcher Derek Lowe and All-Star infielder Nomar Garciaparra, to name only two). Our British hosts probably glazed over as Joe and I rattled on–not about horror novels and crime fiction, but Derek Lowe's durability, J.D. Drew's commitment to the game, and whether or not the BoSox had the stuff to make it to the 2007 World Series (they did, crushing the Colorado Rockies in four games, much to Joe Hill's no doubt considerable delight).

After lunch, we swapped books as our respective publicists dragged us away for more interviews, and I spent the rest of my tour and the long flight home sucking down *Heart-Shaped Box*. I immediately bought *20th Century Ghosts*, and devoured the short stories. Then Chris Ryall dropped the first three *Locke & Key* scripts on me.

When baseball scouts judge player talent, they consider five tools: Hitting for average, hitting for power, how fast the guy can run, how well he can throw, and how well he can catch. The very best players–think A-Rod or Ken Griffey, Jr.–can do it all: Crack a key single when it counts or slam a home run, steal a base, throw out a runner, or make one of those spectacular hauling-ass-back-to-the-ball-over-the-shoulder catches. Most players in the bigs show two or three tools, but the very best players have all five.

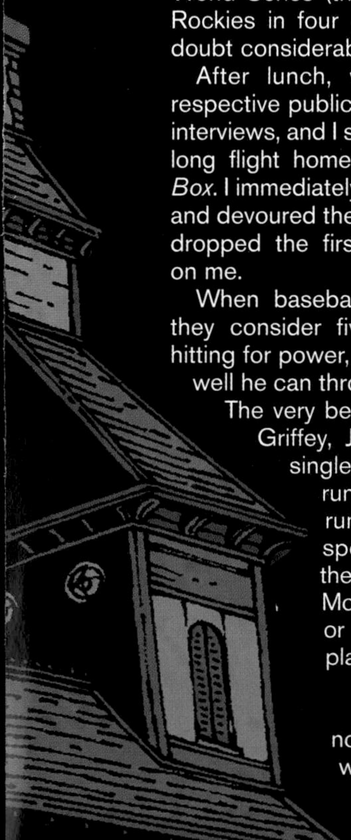

Joe Hill is a five-tool player.

Check it out. A fabulous first novel. The killer short stories, which require a different skill set than writing a novel. And, now, this amazing graphic novel, which is an entirely different form of storytelling than novels or short stories. I'm betting dollars to donuts it won't be long before we see Hill's byline on a major motion picture.

The scripts for the first three issues of *Locke & Key* blew me away. And this was even before Gabriel Rodriguez's stunning art, which has been hauntingly colored by Jay Fotos to achieve exactly the right tone and mood. From Keyhouse's imposing lines to murderer Sam Lesser's listless, watery eyes; in the depiction of Tyler Locke's withdrawal to the pain burned into Kinsey's face, the art and story are perfectly matched to reveal not only the characters, but a steadily mounting tension that will creep you out, surprise you, and is guaranteed to keep you turning the pages.

I read the scripts in a single evening, then pleaded with Ryall for more.

Locke & Key is a graphic novel of the richest kind, presenting a story and characters conceived with all the depth of a full-blown novel, yet perfectly rendered by both writer and artists to take advantage of the graphic medium. Here we have these three lost children–the oldest brother, Tyler, who feels responsible for his father's death; Kinsey, the middle sister, who has already saved her younger brother once, and is now trying to save herself; and six-year-old Bode, who may well be the key, so to speak, to their survival–hauled across the country by their mother after their father is murdered by a homicidal student; these three kids who are at once real because of the secrets they carry, and how the author subtly intertwines their personal stories with the mysteries of Keyhouse and the forces that have drawn them home. (Memo to the Locke family: You want to rebuild your lives, you sure as hell do NOT retreat to a town called Lovecraft.)

Locke & Key works so well, I think, because it resonates with basic fears that all of us share–our loss of innocence; that we might unwittingly hurt someone we love; that revealing ourselves in a moment of weakness might inevitably lead to our undoing. Or worse. This is the stuff of great stories, and when the author tosses in thrills, chills, and the promise of worse things waiting, the reader is in for a helluva ride.

As the Locke family arrives in Lovecraft, Tyler laments that a high school kid can only be one thing–the jock, the slut, the smart kid, or the victim.

If Joe Hill was only one thing, it would be this: An amazing story-teller.

Welcome to Lovecraft.

Welcome to *Locke & Key*.

Welcome to Joe Hill's house.

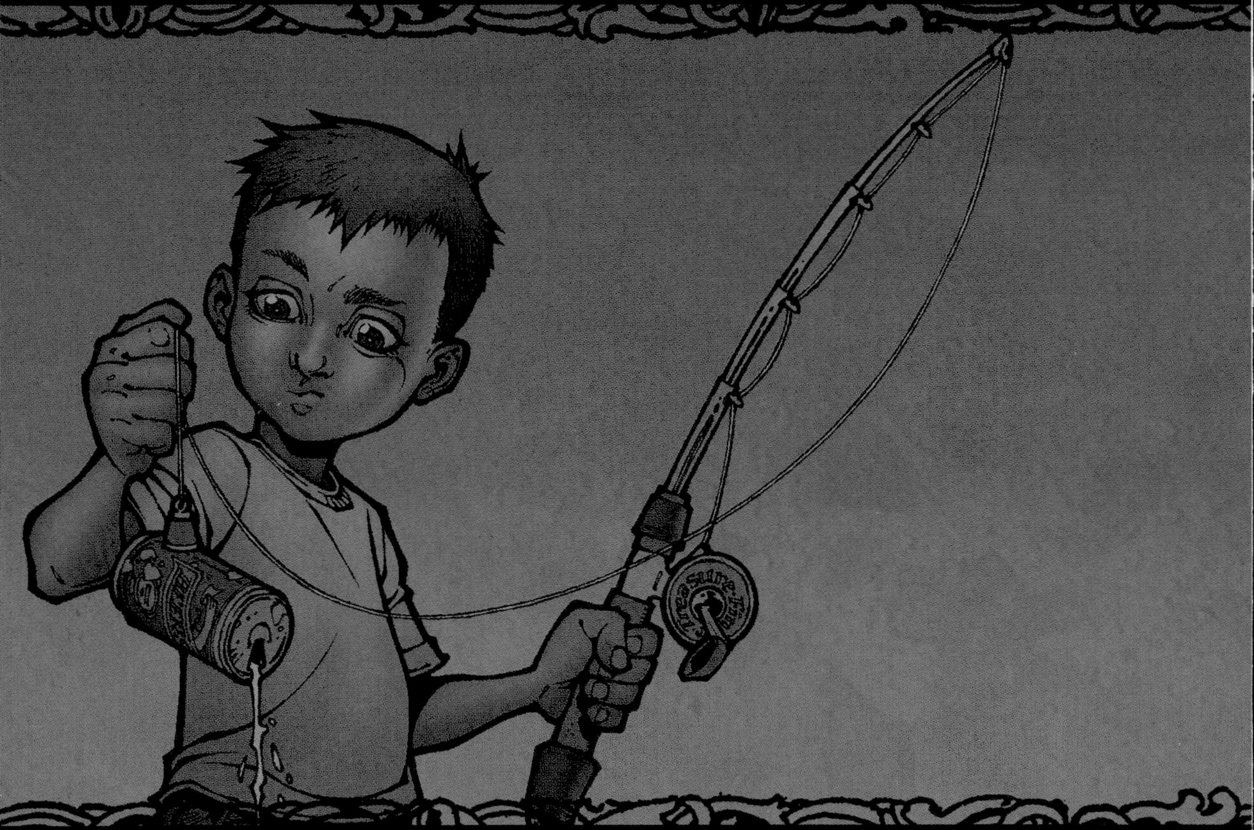

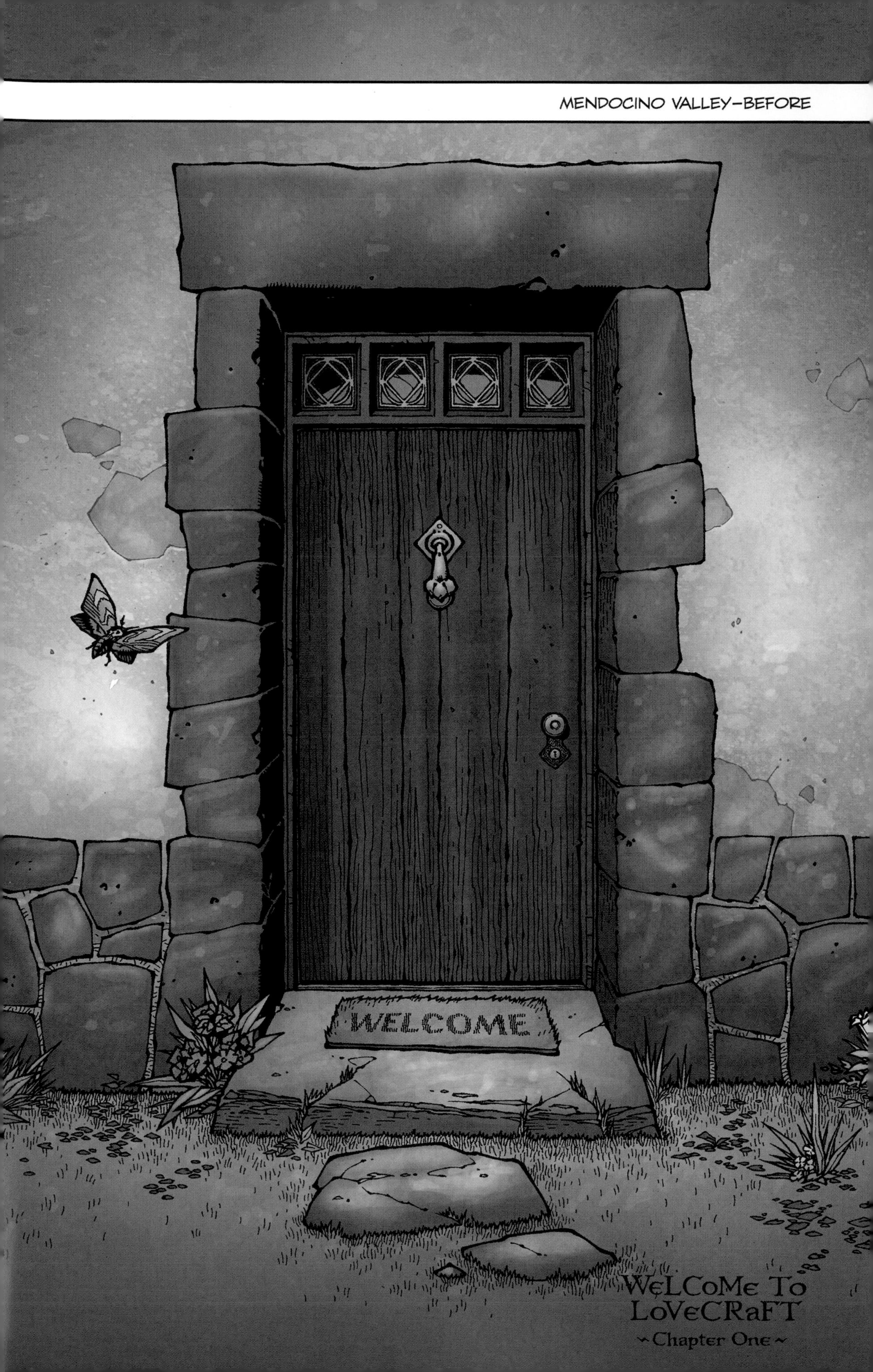
MENDOCINO VALLEY–BEFORE
WELCOME
WELCOME TO LOVECRAFT
~Chapter One~

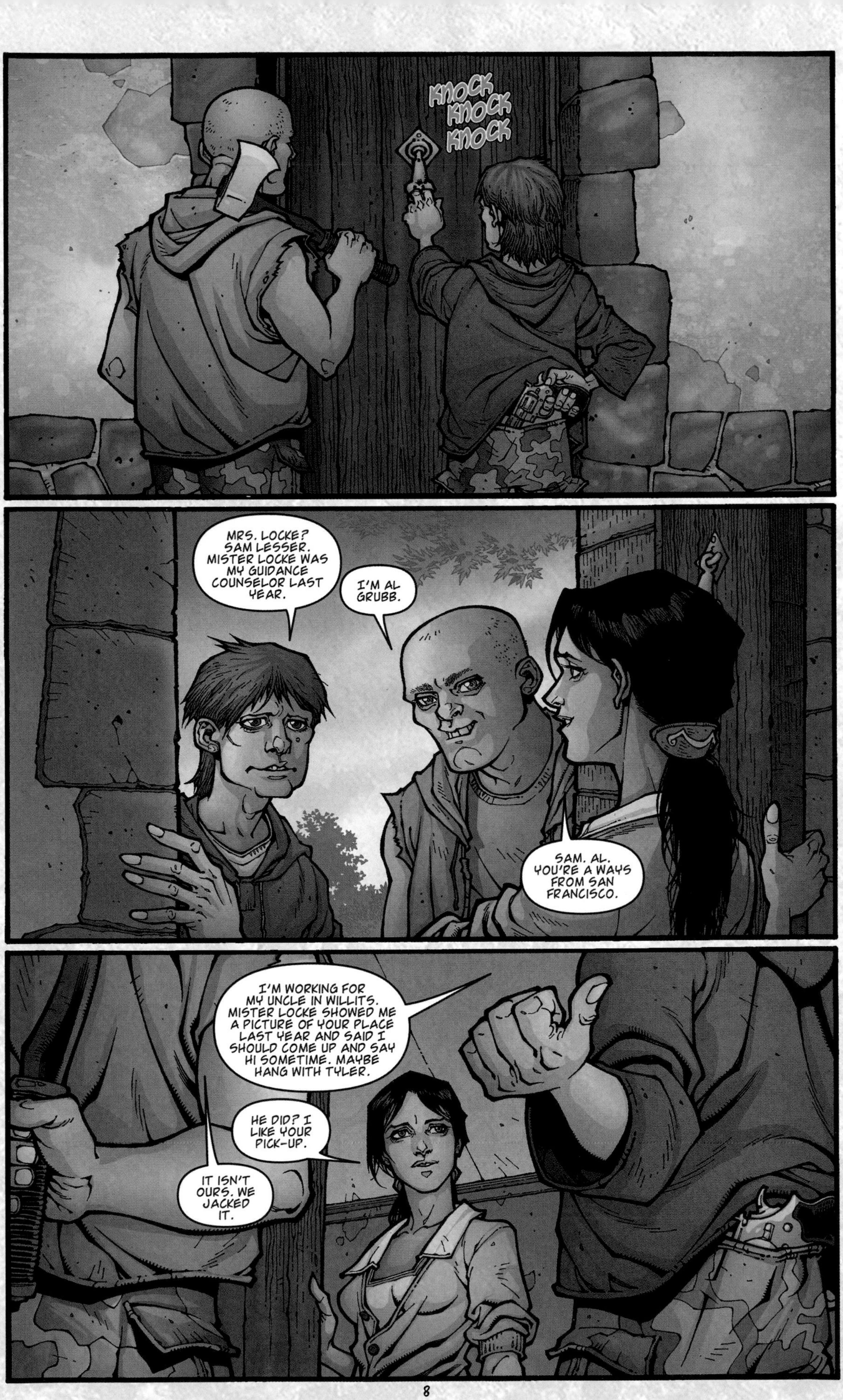
KNOCK KNOCK KNOCK
MRS. LOCKE? SAM LESSER. MISTER LOCKE WAS MY GUIDANCE COUNSELOR LAST YEAR.
I'M AL GRUBB.
SAM. AL. YOU'RE A WAYS FROM SAN FRANCISCO.
I'M WORKING FOR MY UNCLE IN WILLITS. MISTER LOCKE SHOWED ME A PICTURE OF YOUR PLACE LAST YEAR AND SAID I SHOULD COME UP AND SAY HI SOMETIME. MAYBE HANG WITH TYLER.
HE DID? I LIKE YOUR PICK-UP.
IT ISN'T OURS. WE JACKED IT.

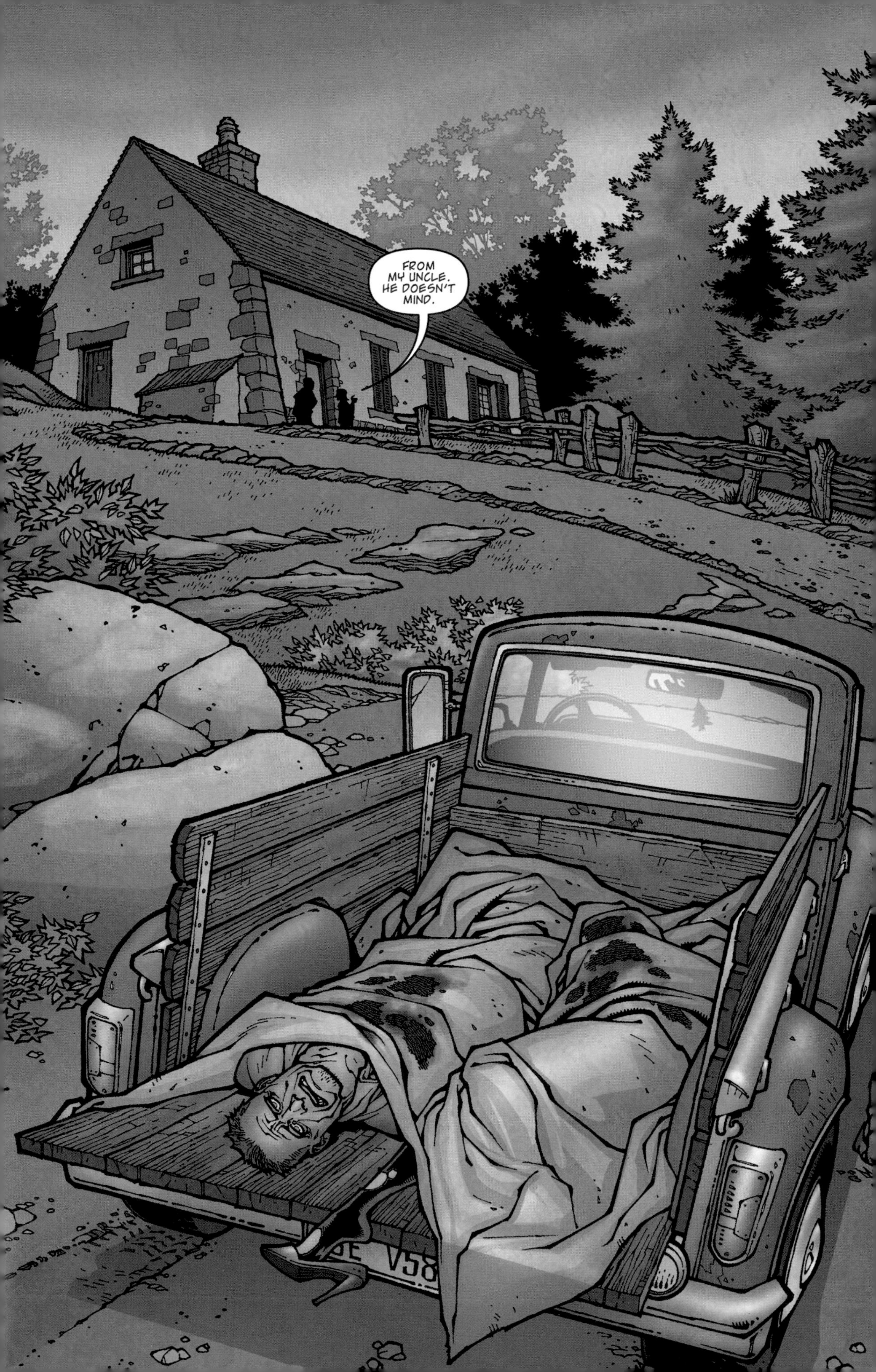
FROM MY UNCLE. HE DOESN'T MIND.

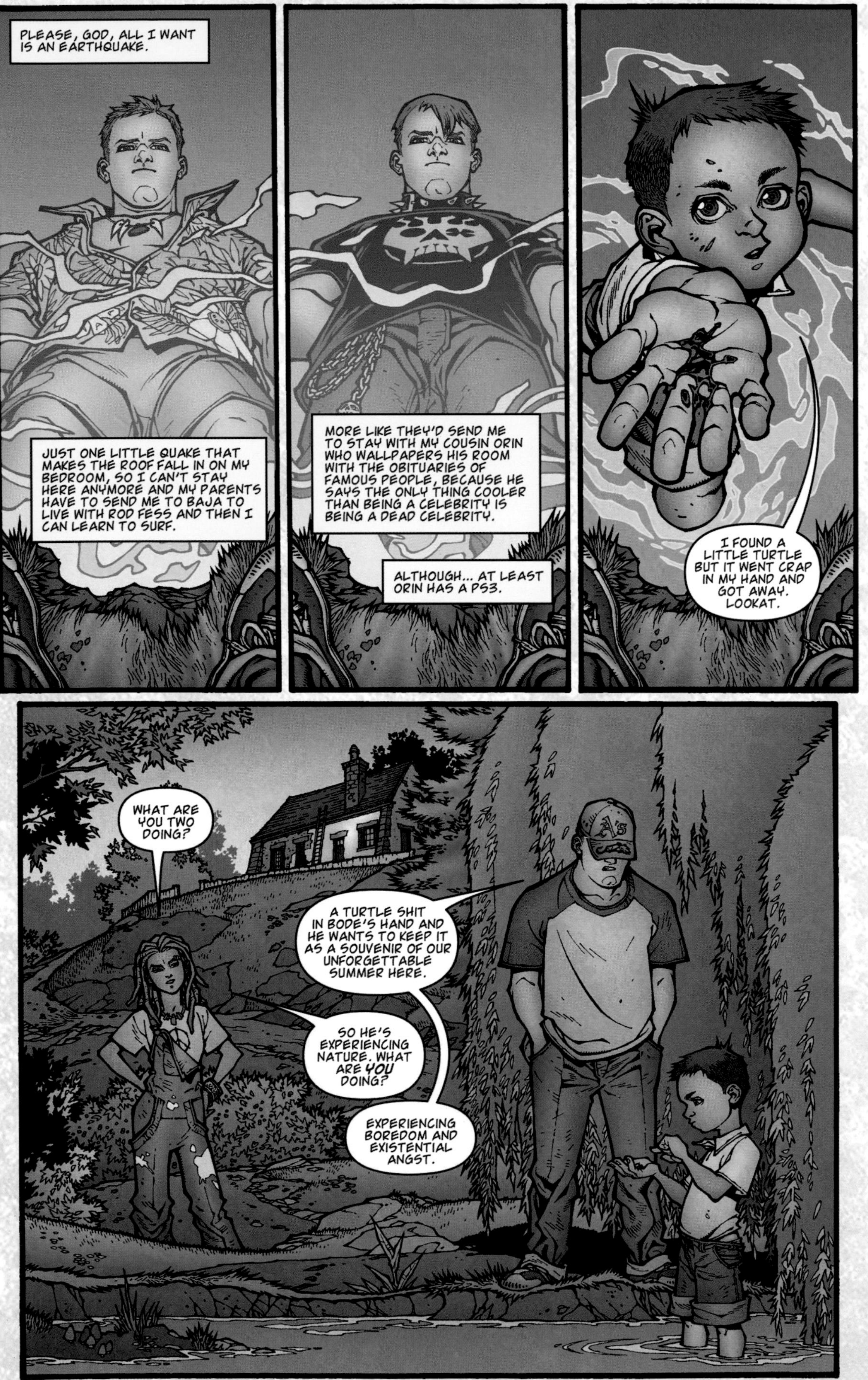
PLEASE, GOD, ALL I WANT IS AN EARTHQUAKE.
JUST ONE LITTLE QUAKE THAT MAKES THE ROOF FALL IN ON MY BEDROOM, SO I CAN'T STAY HERE ANYMORE AND MY PARENTS HAVE TO SEND ME TO BAJA TO LIVE WITH ROD FESS AND THEN I CAN LEARN TO SURF.
MORE LIKE THEY'D SEND ME TO STAY WITH MY COUSIN ORIN WHO WALLPAPERS HIS ROOM WITH THE OBITUARIES OF FAMOUS PEOPLE, BECAUSE HE SAYS THE ONLY THING COOLER THAN BEING A CELEBRITY IS BEING A DEAD CELEBRITY.
ALTHOUGH... AT LEAST ORIN HAS A PS3.
I FOUND A LITTLE TURTLE BUT IT WENT CRAP IN MY HAND AND GOT AWAY. LOOKAT.
WHAT ARE YOU TWO DOING?
A TURTLE SHIT IN BODE'S HAND AND HE WANTS TO KEEP IT AS A SOUVENIR OF OUR UNFORGETTABLE SUMMER HERE.
SO HE'S EXPERIENCING NATURE. WHAT ARE *YOU* DOING?
EXPERIENCING BOREDOM AND EXISTENTIAL ANGST.

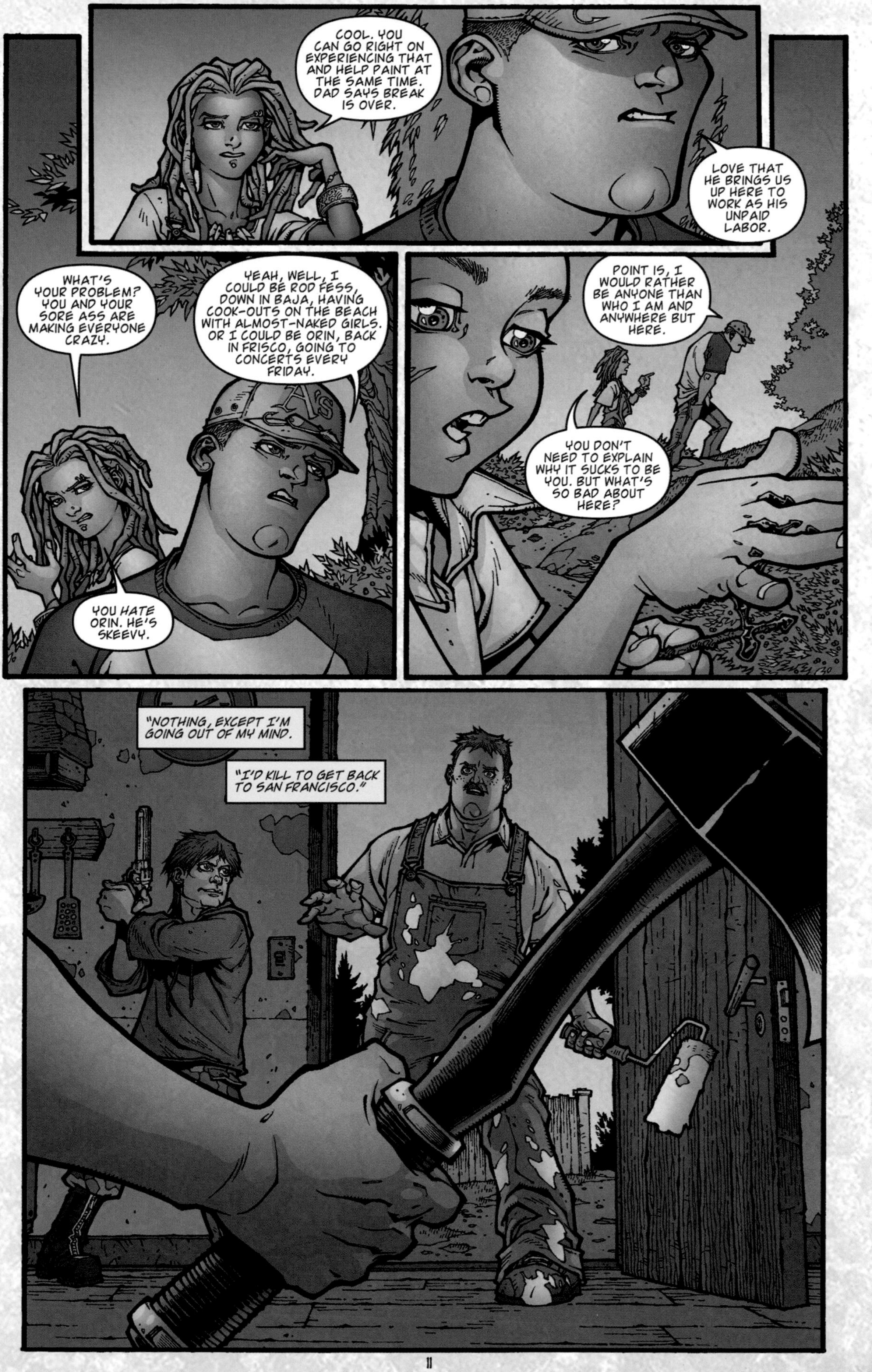
COOL. YOU CAN GO RIGHT ON EXPERIENCING THAT AND HELP PAINT AT THE SAME TIME. DAD SAYS BREAK IS OVER.
LOVE THAT HE BRINGS US UP HERE TO WORK AS HIS UNPAID LABOR.
WHAT'S YOUR PROBLEM? YOU AND YOUR SORE ASS ARE MAKING EVERYONE CRAZY.
YEAH, WELL, I COULD BE ROD FESS, DOWN IN BAJA, HAVING COOK-OUTS ON THE BEACH WITH ALMOST-NAKED GIRLS. OR I COULD BE ORIN, BACK IN FRISCO, GOING TO CONCERTS EVERY FRIDAY.
YOU HATE ORIN. HE'S SKEEVY.
POINT IS, I WOULD RATHER BE ANYONE THAN WHO I AM AND ANYWHERE BUT HERE.
YOU DON'T NEED TO EXPLAIN WHY IT SUCKS TO BE YOU. BUT WHAT'S SO BAD ABOUT HERE?
"NOTHING, EXCEPT I'M GOING OUT OF MY MIND.
"I'D KILL TO GET BACK TO SAN FRANCISCO."

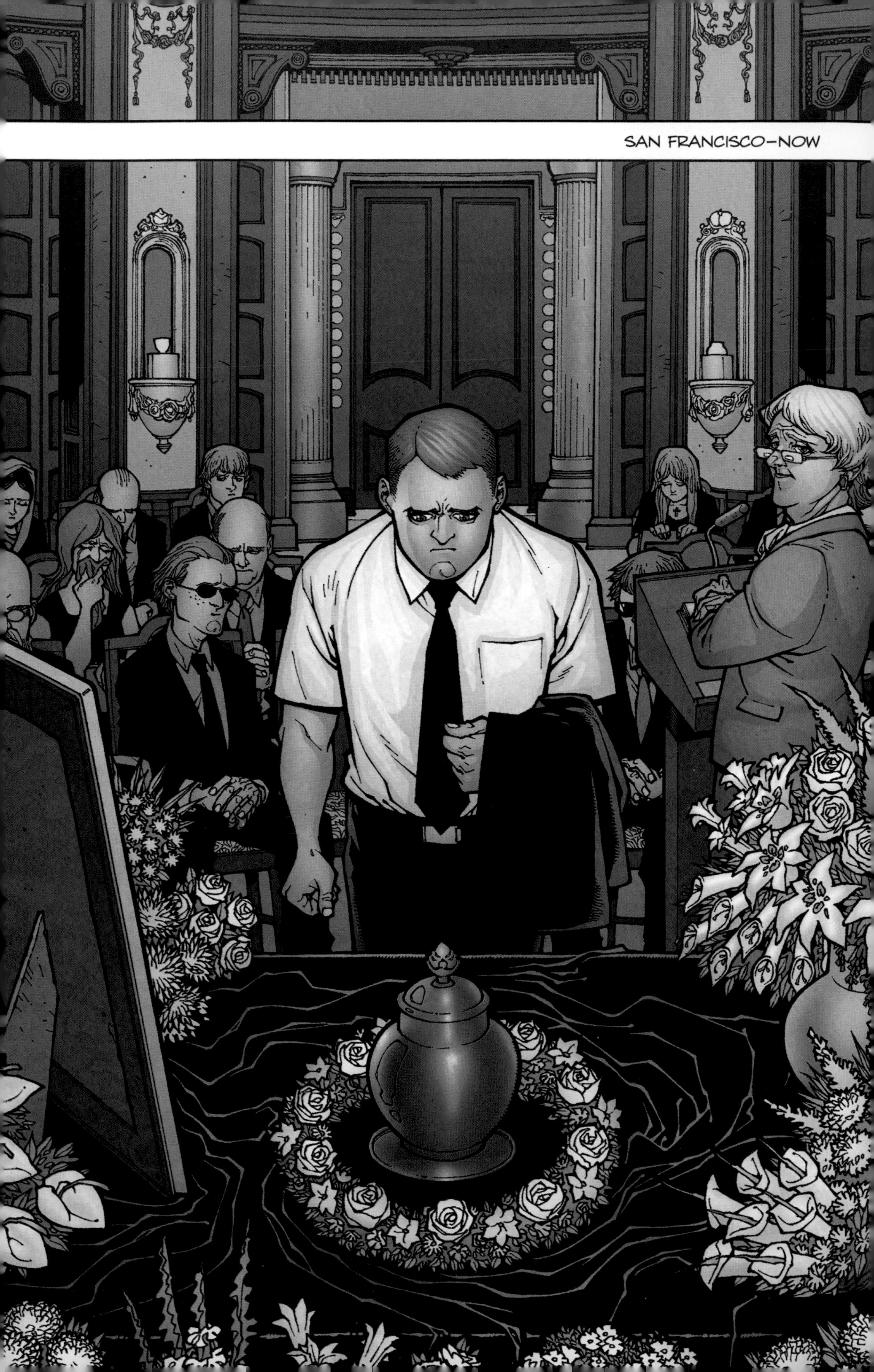
SAN FRANCISCO—NOW

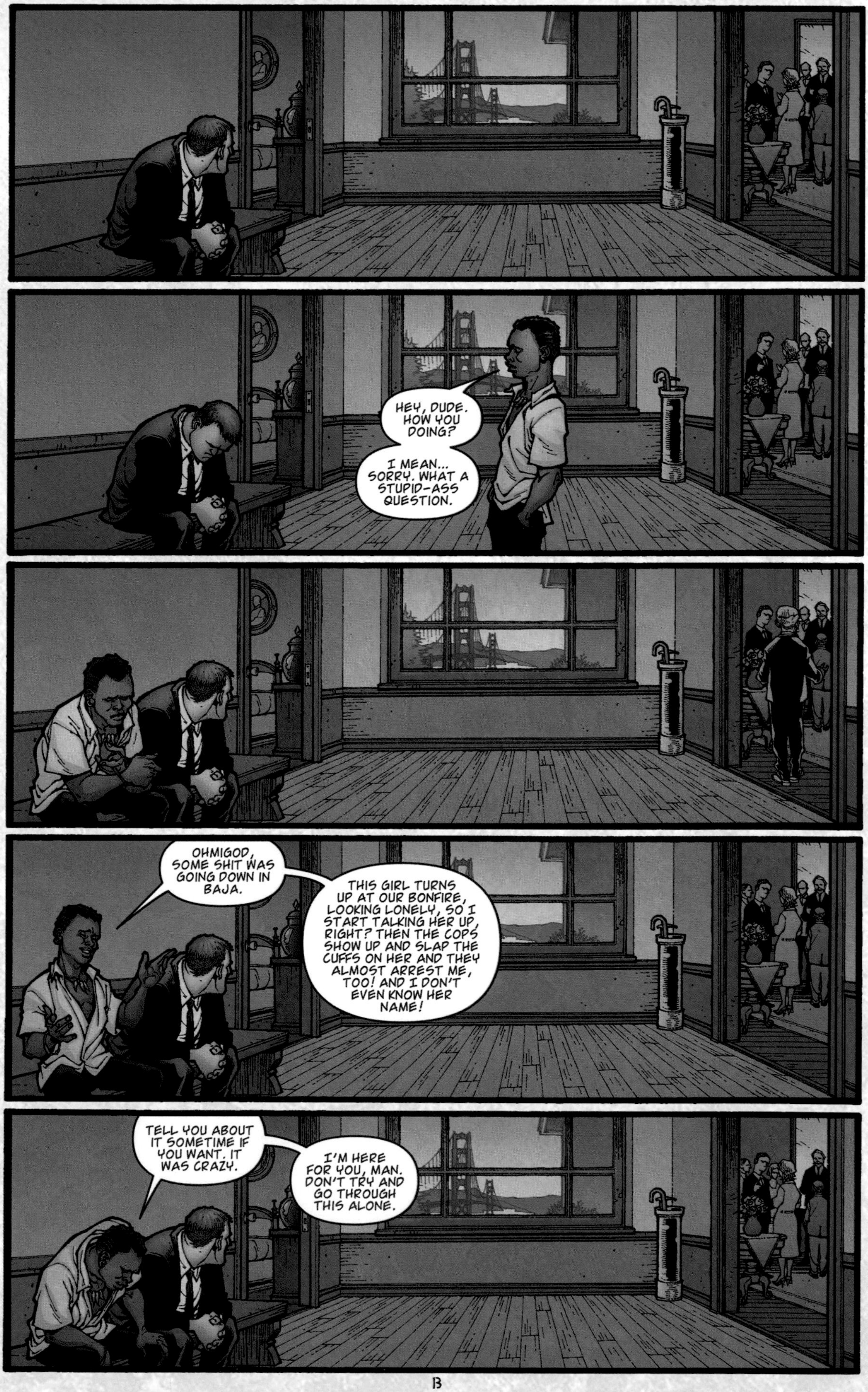
HEY, DUDE. HOW YOU DOING?
I MEAN... SORRY. WHAT A STUPID-ASS QUESTION.
OHMIGOD, SOME SHIT WAS GOING DOWN IN BAJA.
THIS GIRL TURNS UP AT OUR BONFIRE, LOOKING LONELY, SO I START TALKING HER UP, RIGHT? THEN THE COPS SHOW UP AND SLAP THE CUFFS ON HER AND THEY ALMOST ARREST ME, TOO! AND I DON'T EVEN KNOW HER NAME!
TELL YOU ABOUT IT SOMETIME IF YOU WANT. IT WAS CRAZY.
I'M HERE FOR YOU, MAN. DON'T TRY AND GO THROUGH THIS ALONE.

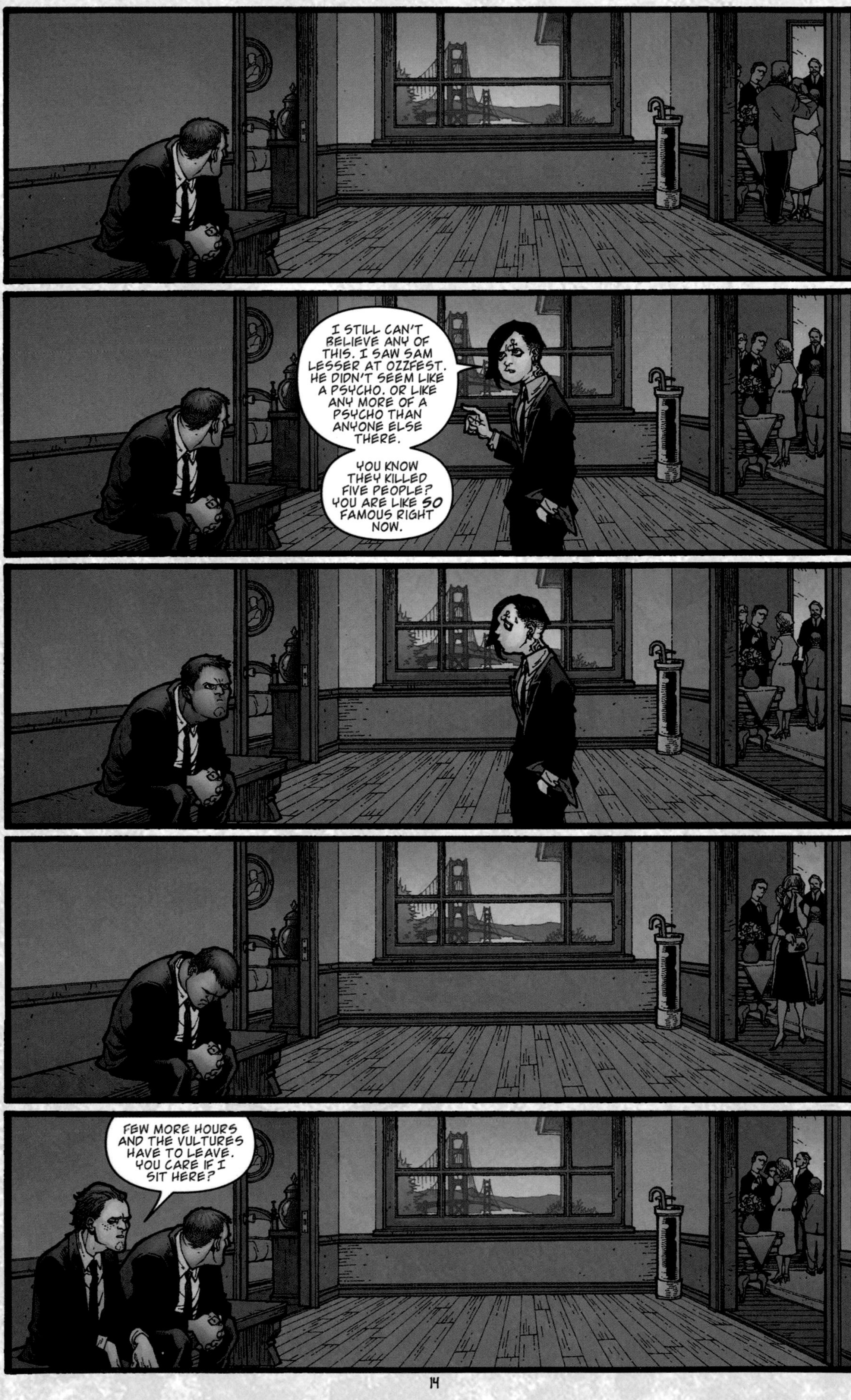
I STILL CAN'T BELIEVE ANY OF THIS. I SAW SAM LESSER AT OZZFEST. HE DIDN'T SEEM LIKE A PSYCHO. OR LIKE ANY MORE OF A PSYCHO THAN ANYONE ELSE THERE.
YOU KNOW THEY KILLED FIVE PEOPLE? YOU ARE LIKE SO FAMOUS RIGHT NOW.
FEW MORE HOURS AND THE VULTURES HAVE TO LEAVE. YOU CARE IF I SIT HERE?

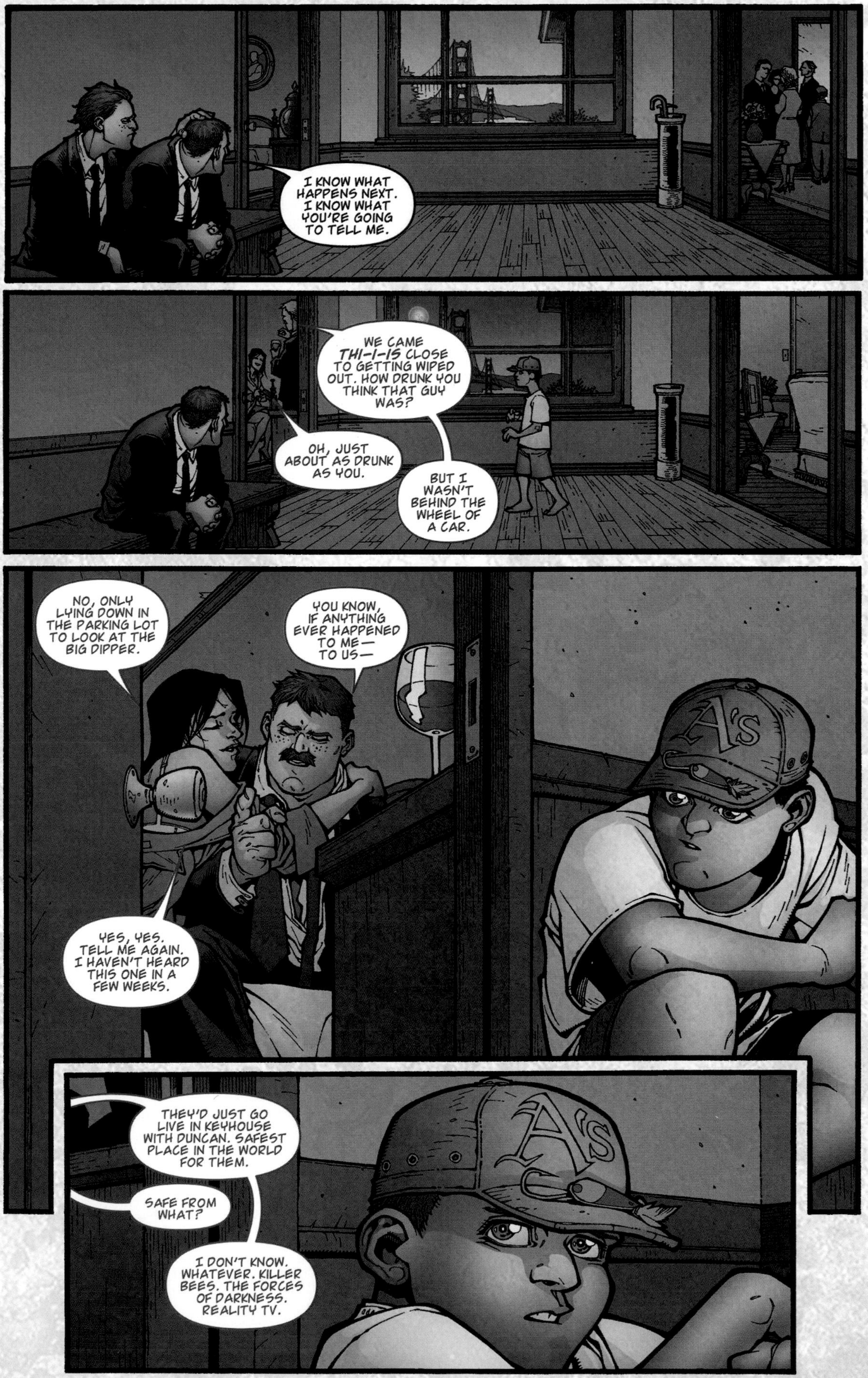
I KNOW WHAT HAPPENS NEXT. I KNOW WHAT YOU'RE GOING TO TELL ME.
WE CAME *THI-I-IS* CLOSE TO GETTING WIPED OUT. HOW DRUNK YOU THINK THAT GUY WAS?
OH, JUST ABOUT AS DRUNK AS YOU.
BUT I WASN'T BEHIND THE WHEEL OF A CAR.
NO, ONLY LYING DOWN IN THE PARKING LOT TO LOOK AT THE BIG DIPPER.
YOU KNOW, IF ANYTHING EVER HAPPENED TO ME— TO US—
YES, YES. TELL ME AGAIN. I HAVEN'T HEARD THIS ONE IN A FEW WEEKS.
THEY'D JUST GO LIVE IN KEYHOUSE WITH DUNCAN. SAFEST PLACE IN THE WORLD FOR THEM.
SAFE FROM WHAT?
I DON'T KNOW. WHATEVER. KILLER BEES. THE FORCES OF DARKNESS. REALITY TV.

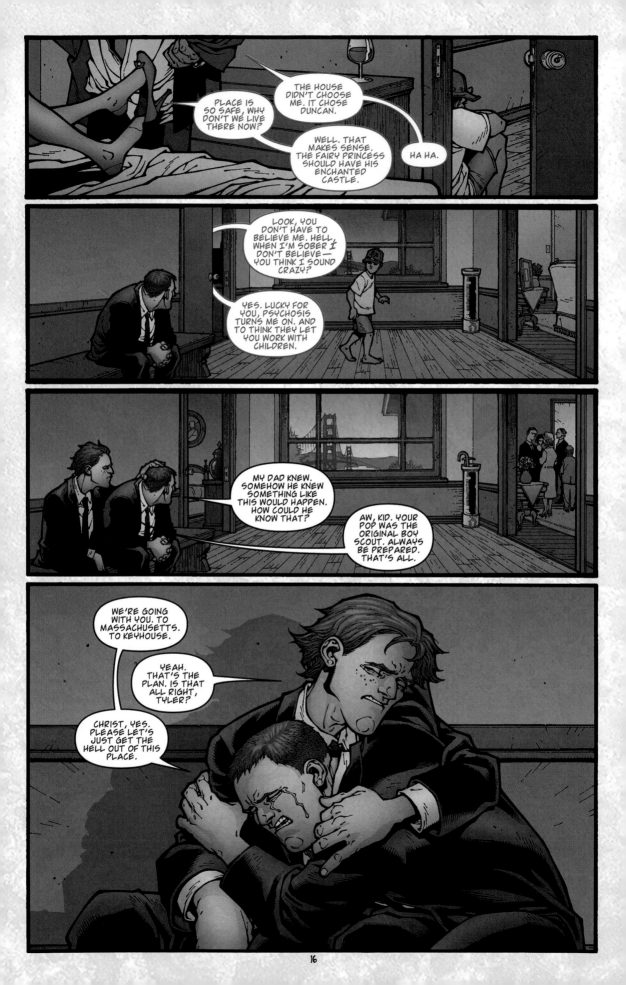

16

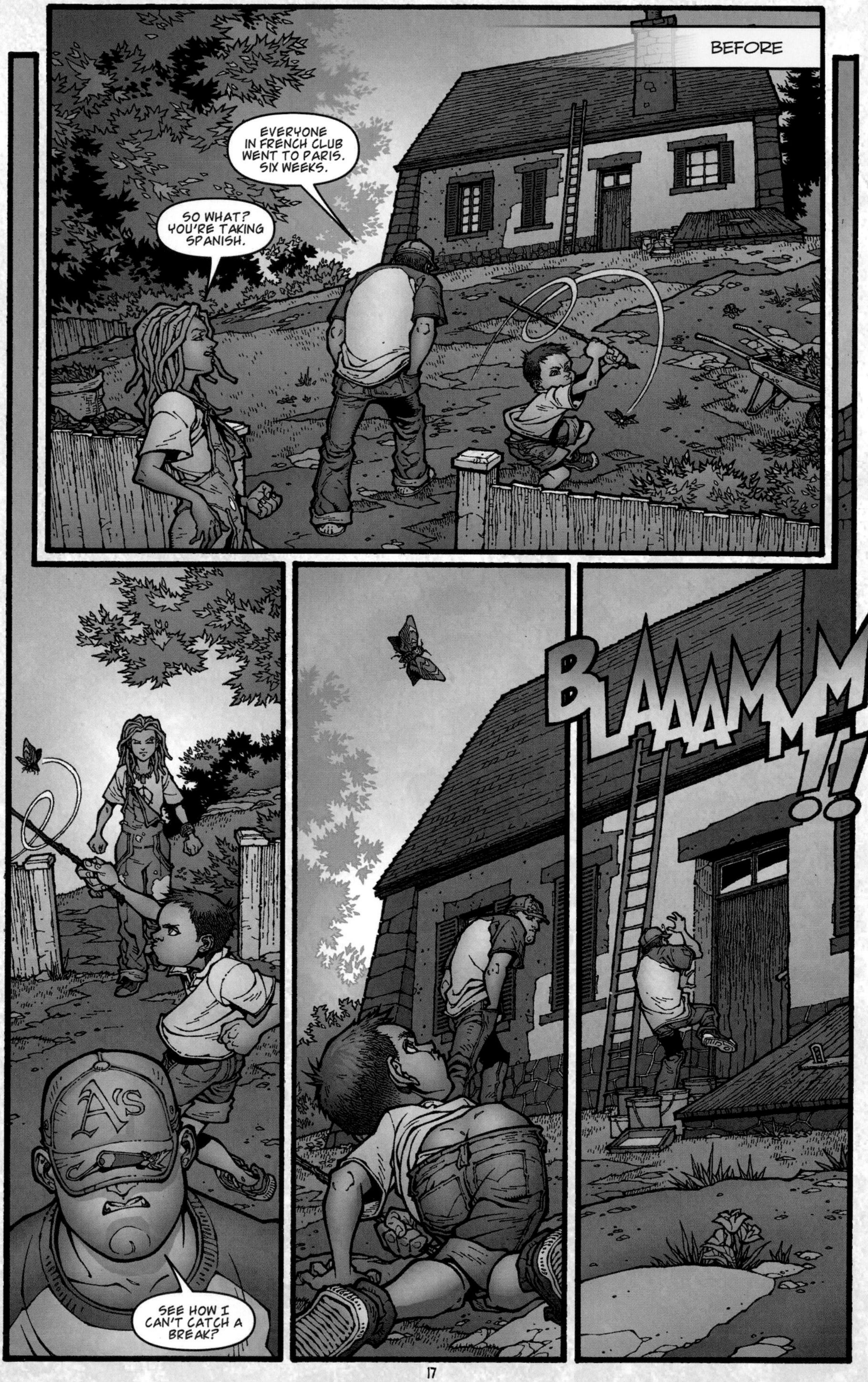
BEFORE
EVERYONE IN FRENCH CLUB WENT TO PARIS. SIX WEEKS.
SO WHAT? YOU'RE TAKING SPANISH.
SEE HOW I CAN'T CATCH A BREAK?
BLAAAMMM!!

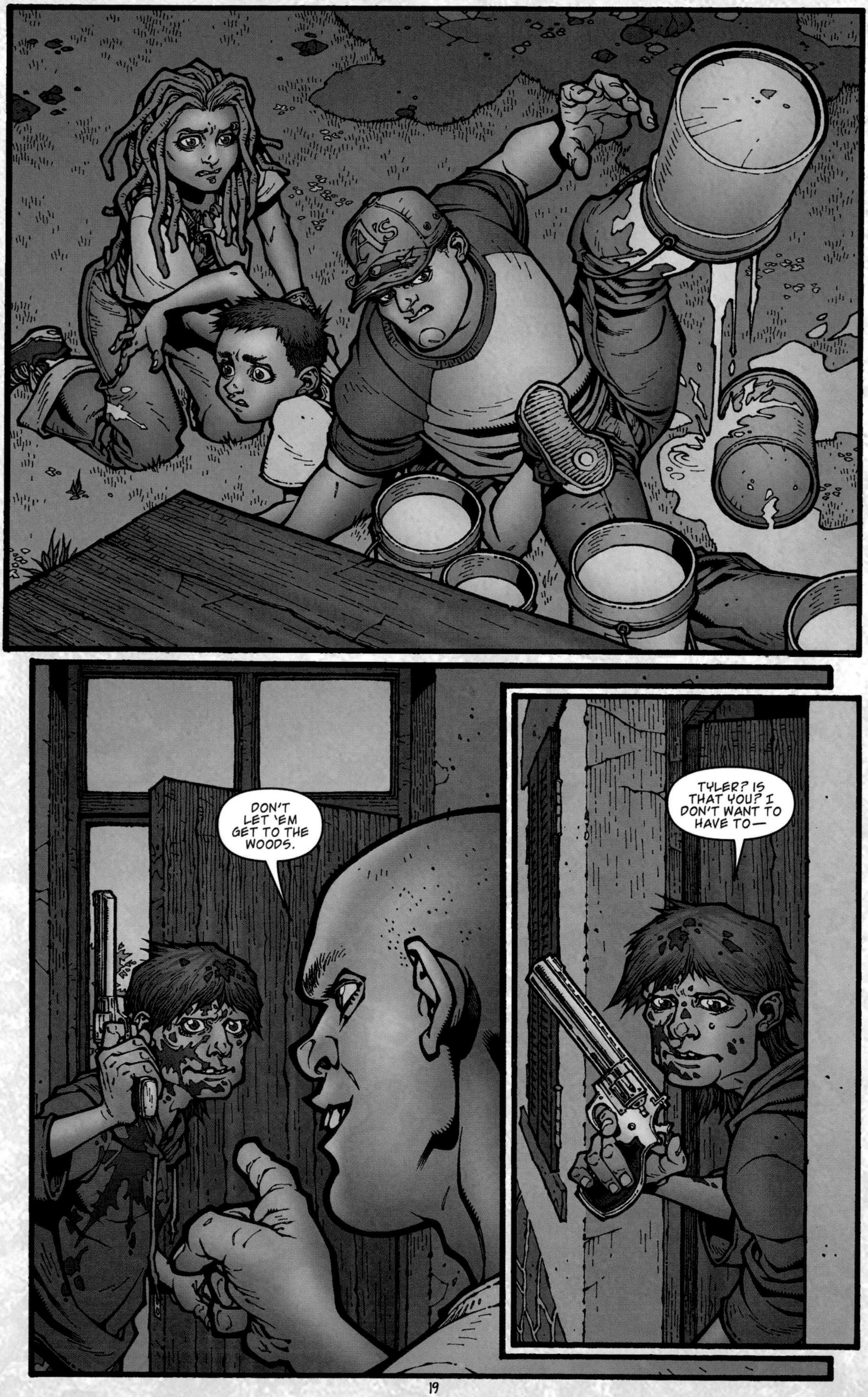
DON'T LET 'EM GET TO THE WOODS.
TYLER? IS THAT YOU? I DON'T WANT TO HAVE TO—

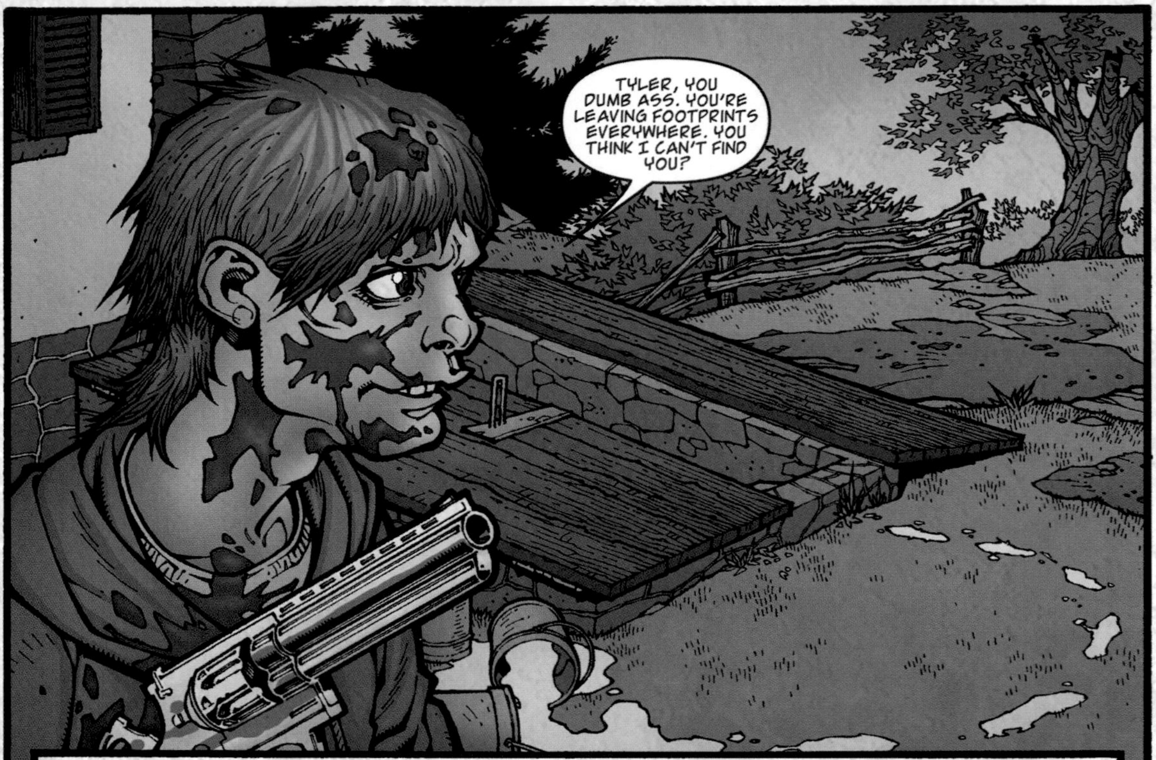
TYLER, YOU DUMB ASS. YOU'RE LEAVING FOOTPRINTS EVERYWHERE. YOU THINK I CAN'T FIND YOU?

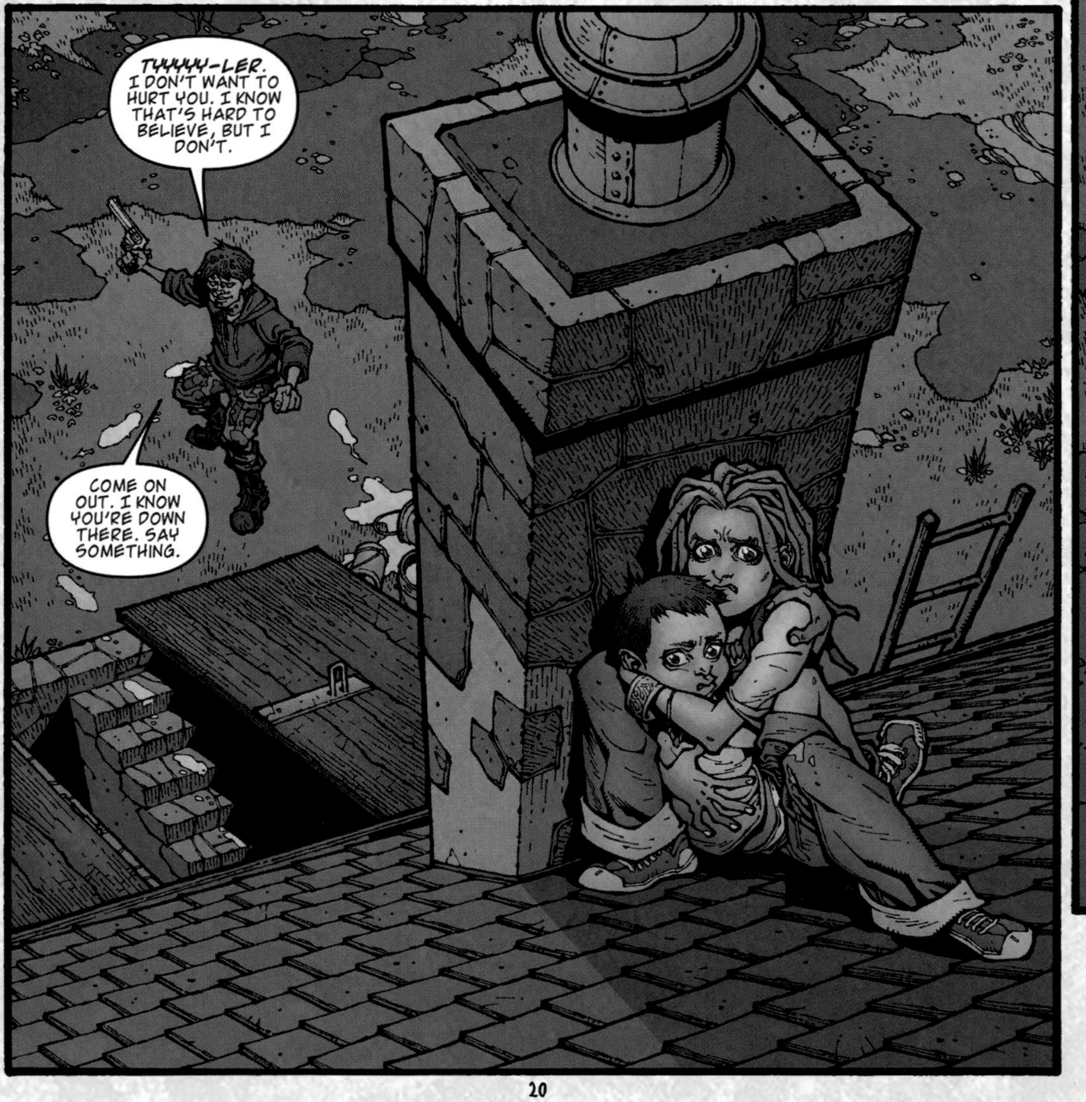
TYYYYY-LER. I DON'T WANT TO HURT YOU. I KNOW THAT'S HARD TO BELIEVE, BUT I DON'T.
COME ON OUT. I KNOW YOU'RE DOWN THERE. SAY SOMETHING.

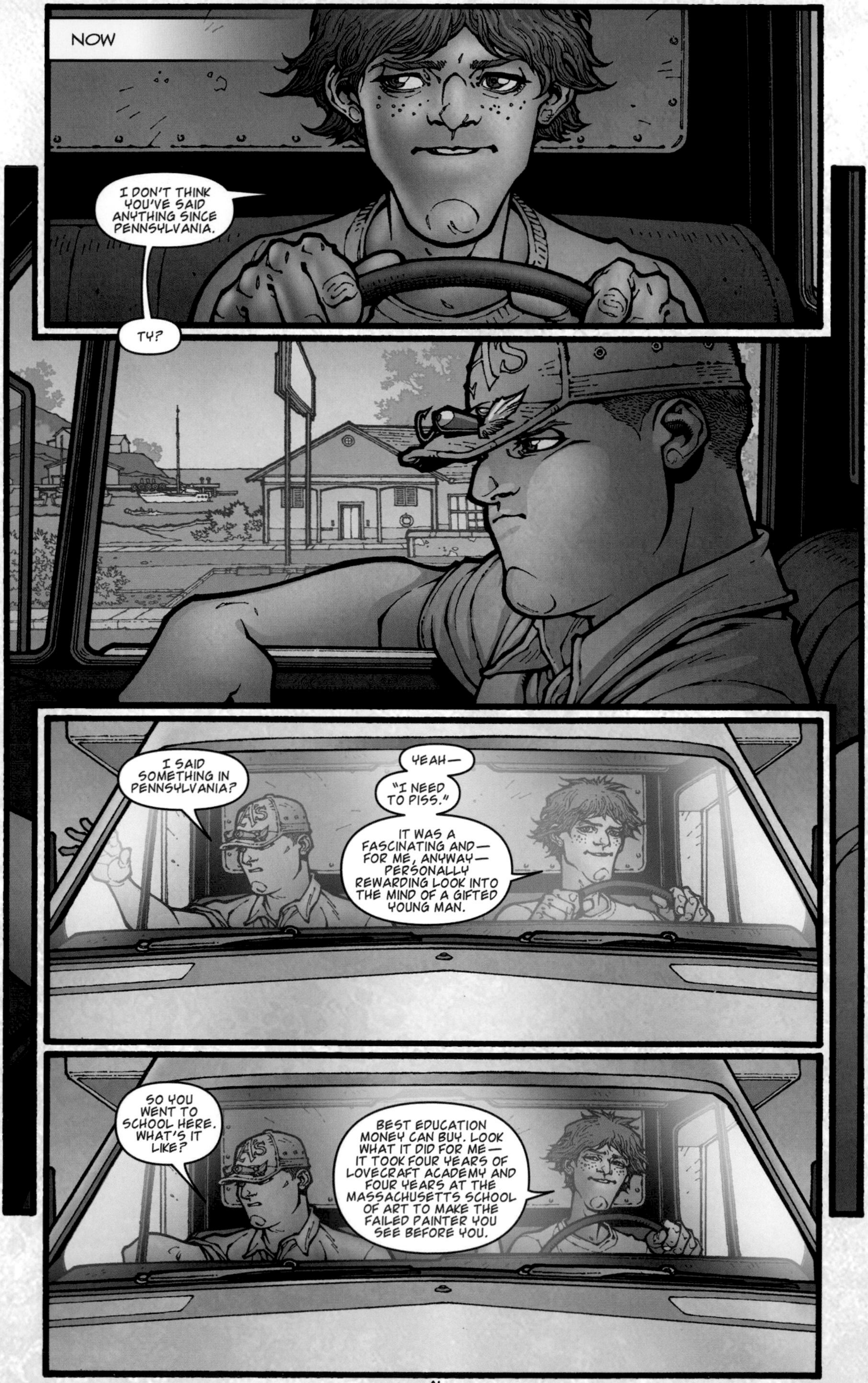
NOW
I DON'T THINK YOU'VE SAID ANYTHING SINCE PENNSYLVANIA.
TY?
I SAID SOMETHING IN PENNSYLVANIA?
YEAH—
"I NEED TO PISS."
IT WAS A FASCINATING AND— FOR ME, ANYWAY— PERSONALLY REWARDING LOOK INTO THE MIND OF A GIFTED YOUNG MAN.
SO YOU WENT TO SCHOOL HERE. WHAT'S IT LIKE?
BEST EDUCATION MONEY CAN BUY. LOOK WHAT IT DID FOR ME— IT TOOK FOUR YEARS OF LOVECRAFT ACADEMY AND FOUR YEARS AT THE MASSACHUSETTS SCHOOL OF ART TO MAKE THE FAILED PAINTER YOU SEE BEFORE YOU.

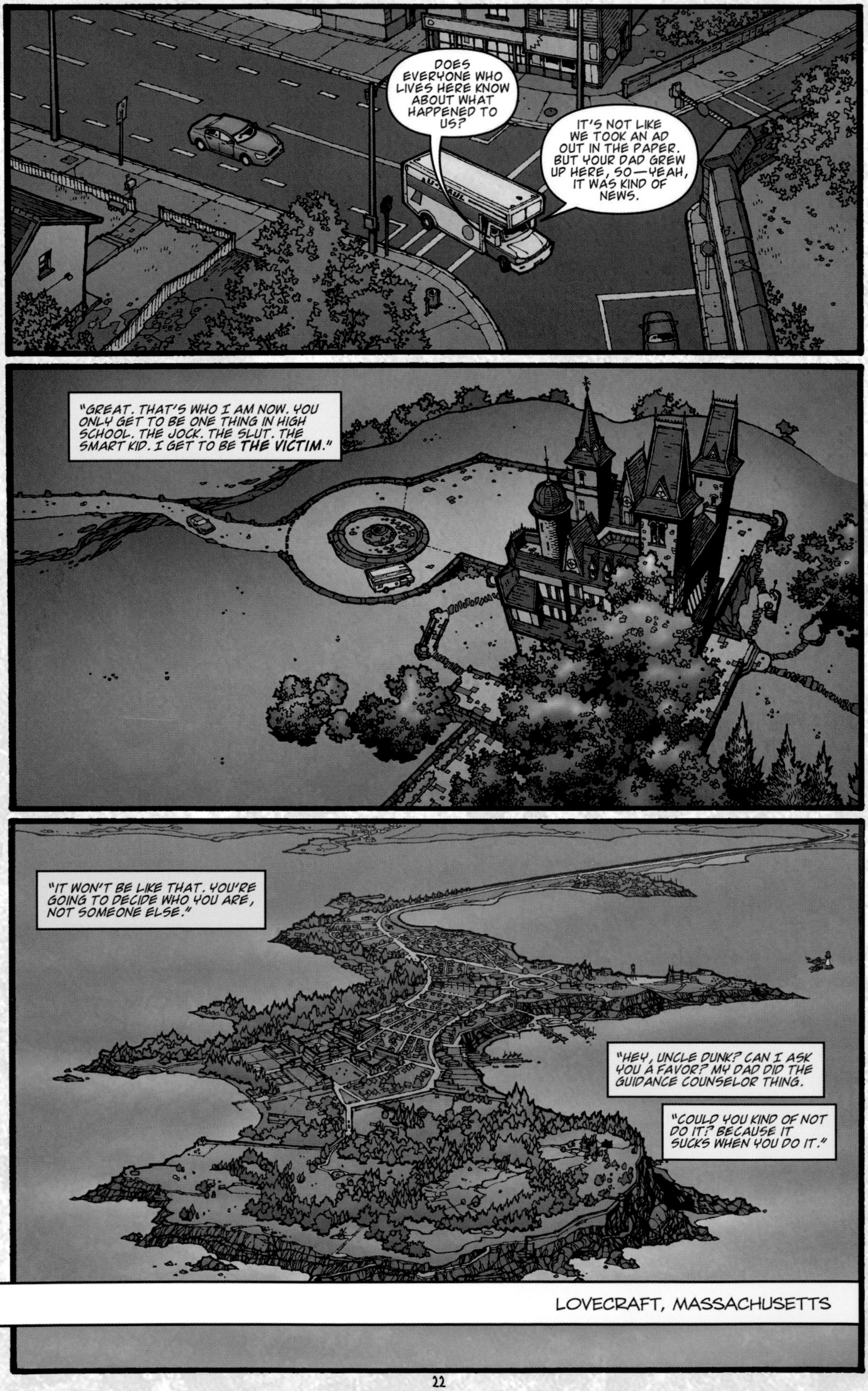
DOES EVERYONE WHO LIVES HERE KNOW ABOUT WHAT HAPPENED TO US?
IT'S NOT LIKE WE TOOK AN AD OUT IN THE PAPER. BUT YOUR DAD GREW UP HERE, SO—YEAH, IT WAS KIND OF NEWS.
"GREAT. THAT'S WHO I AM NOW. YOU ONLY GET TO BE ONE THING IN HIGH SCHOOL. THE JOCK. THE SLUT. THE SMART KID. I GET TO BE THE VICTIM."
"IT WON'T BE LIKE THAT. YOU'RE GOING TO DECIDE WHO YOU ARE, NOT SOMEONE ELSE."
"HEY, UNCLE DUNK? CAN I ASK YOU A FAVOR? MY DAD DID THE GUIDANCE COUNSELOR THING.
"COULD YOU KIND OF NOT DO IT? BECAUSE IT SUCKS WHEN YOU DO IT."
LOVECRAFT, MASSACHUSETTS

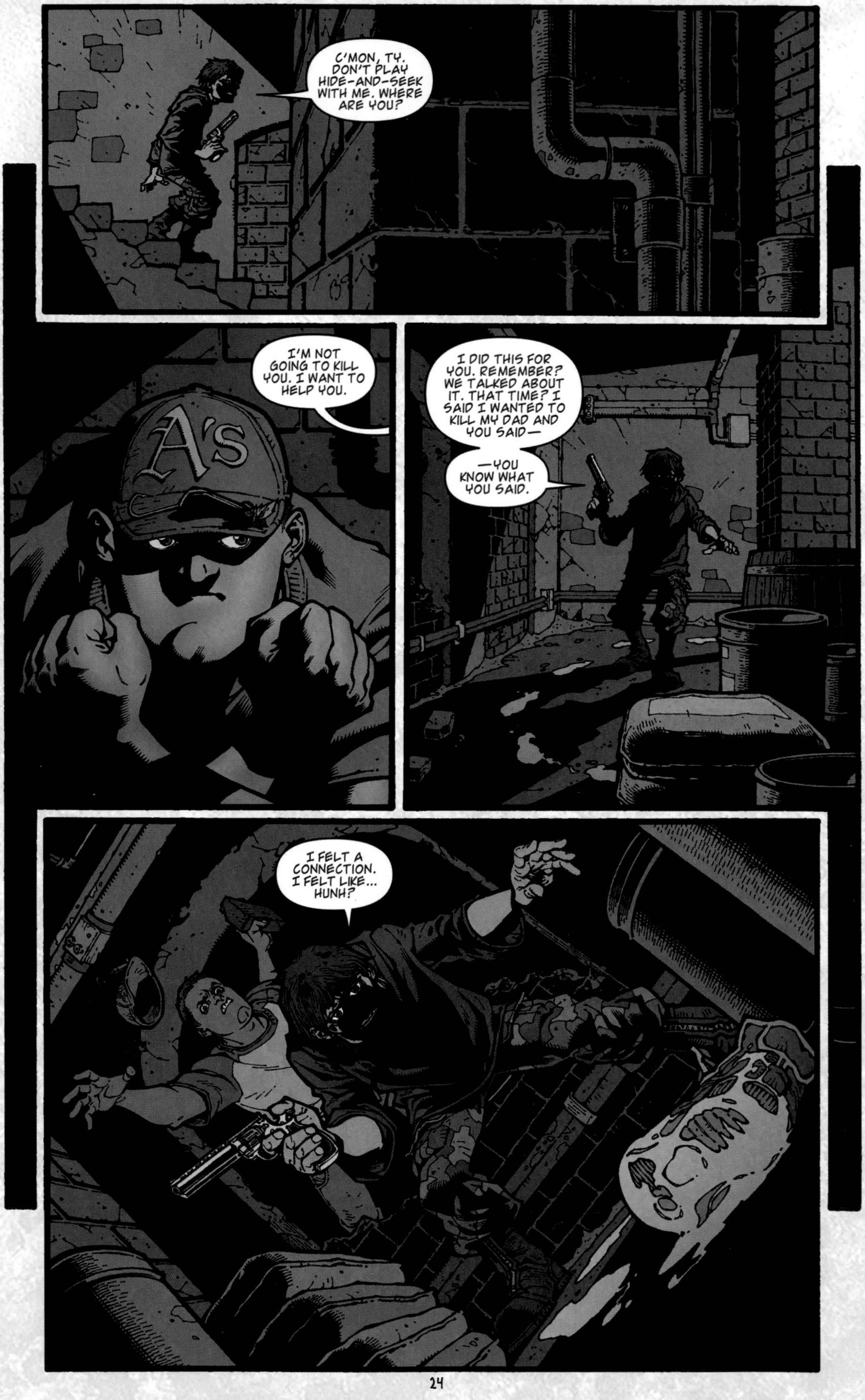
C'MON, TY. DON'T PLAY HIDE-AND-SEEK WITH ME. WHERE ARE YOU?
I'M NOT GOING TO KILL YOU. I WANT TO HELP YOU.
I DID THIS FOR YOU. REMEMBER? WE TALKED ABOUT IT. THAT TIME? I SAID I WANTED TO KILL MY DAD AND YOU SAID—
—YOU KNOW WHAT YOU SAID.
I FELT A CONNECTION. I FELT LIKE... HUNH?

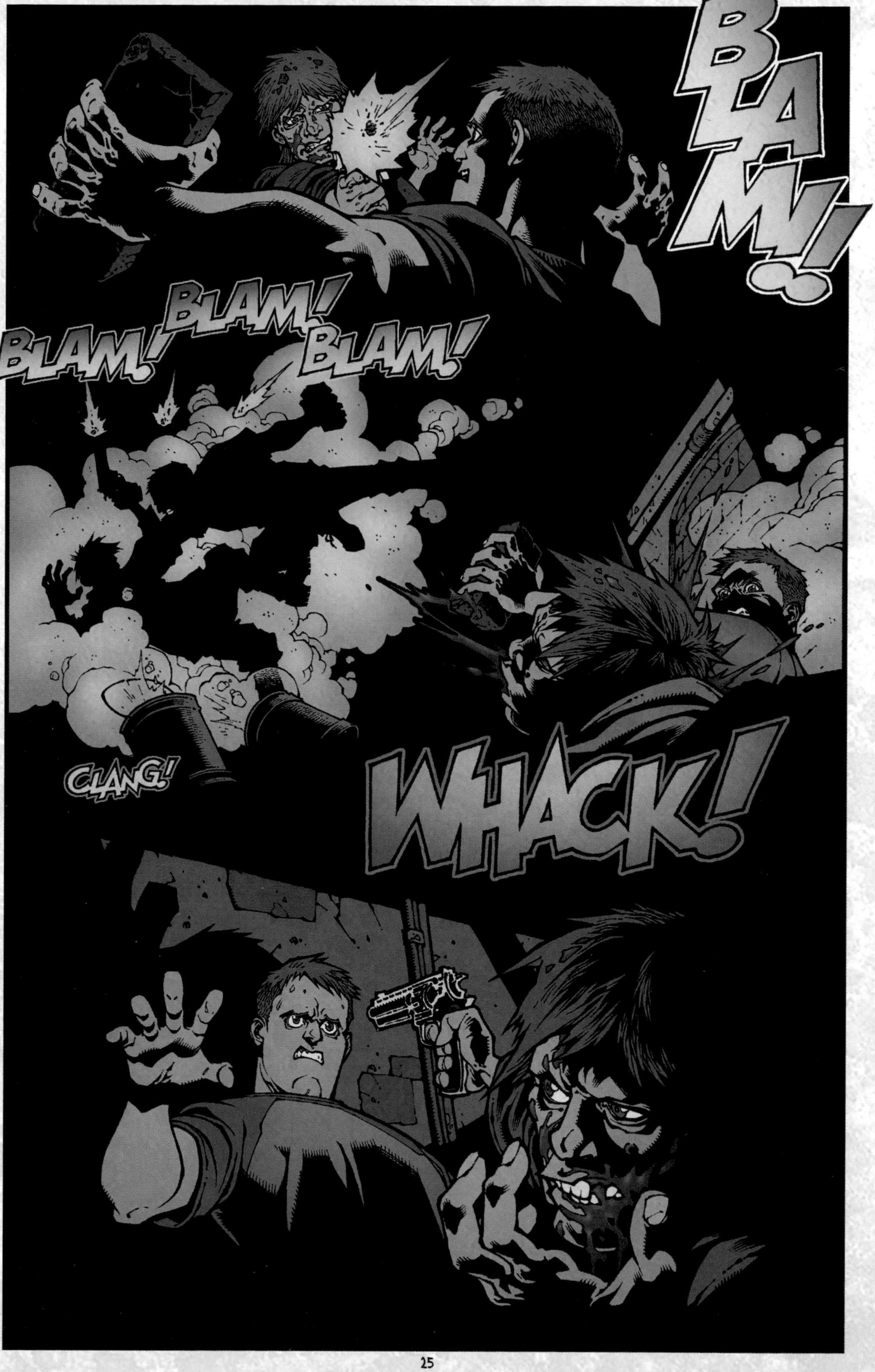
BLAM!
BLAM! BLAM! BLAM!
CLANG!
WHACK!

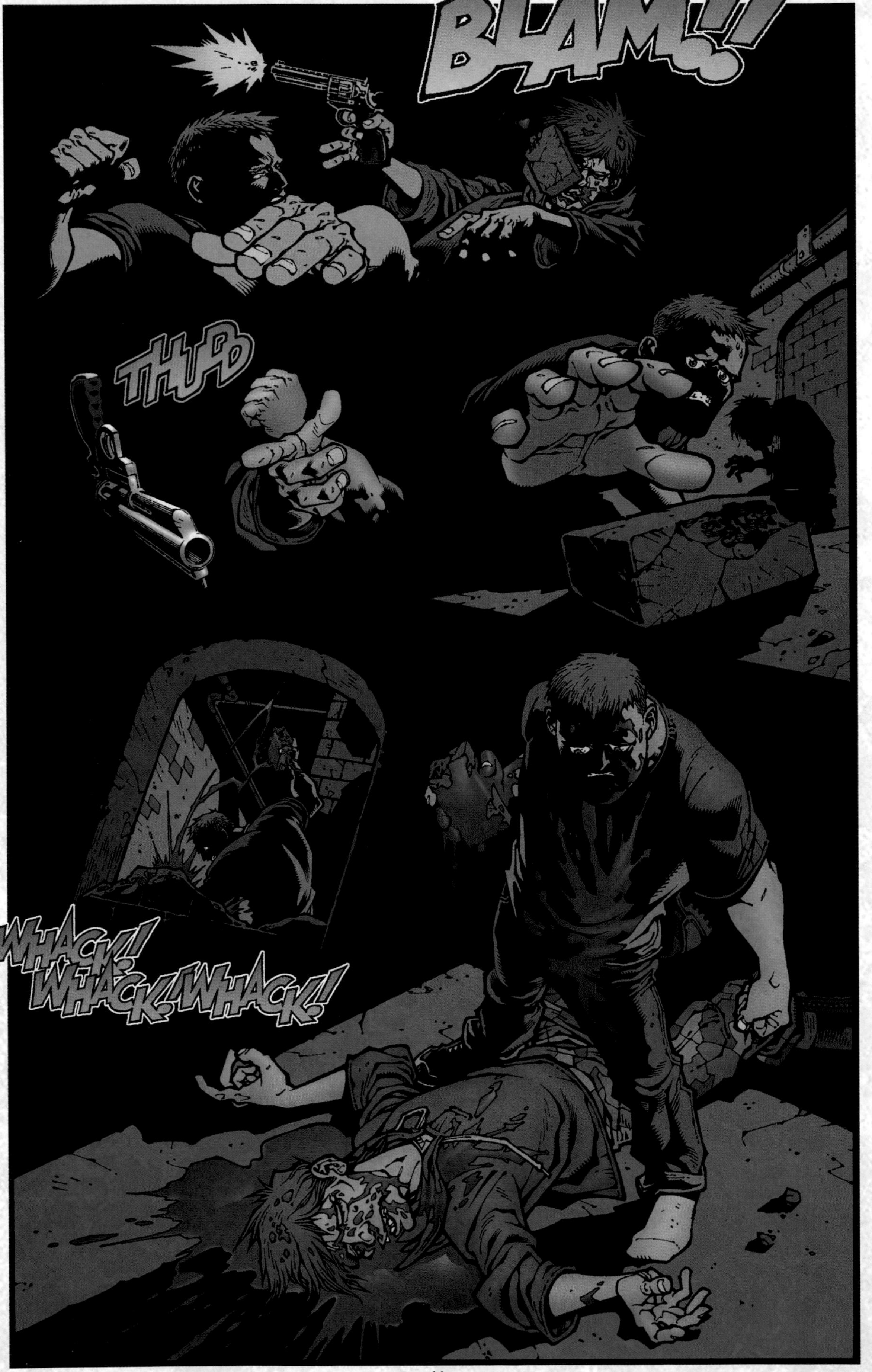
BLAM!!
THUD
WHACK! WHACK! WHACK!

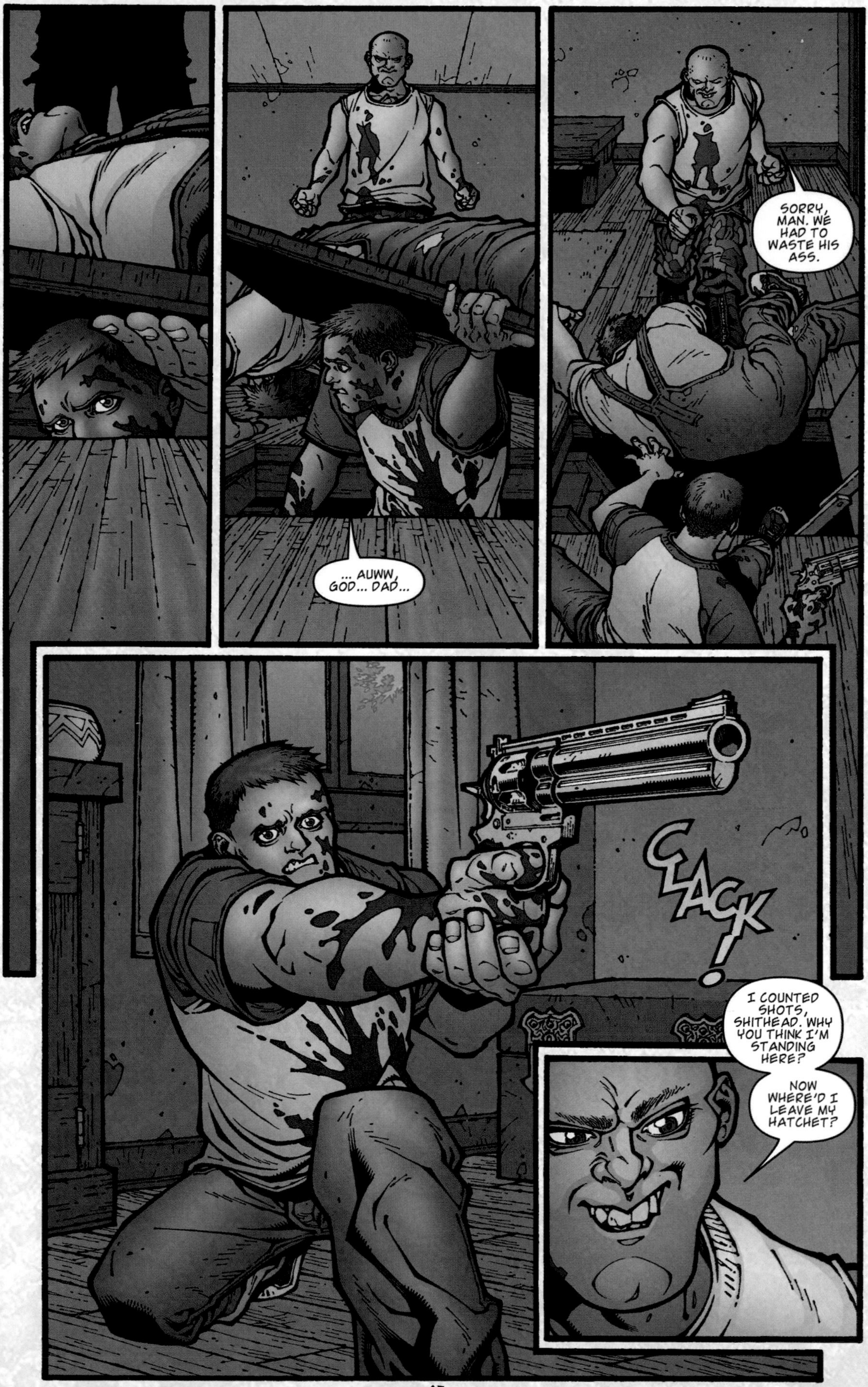
... AUWW, GOD... DAD...
SORRY, MAN. WE HAD TO WASTE HIS ASS.
CLACK!
I COUNTED SHOTS, SHITHEAD. WHY YOU THINK I'M STANDING HERE?
NOW WHERE'D I LEAVE MY HATCHET?

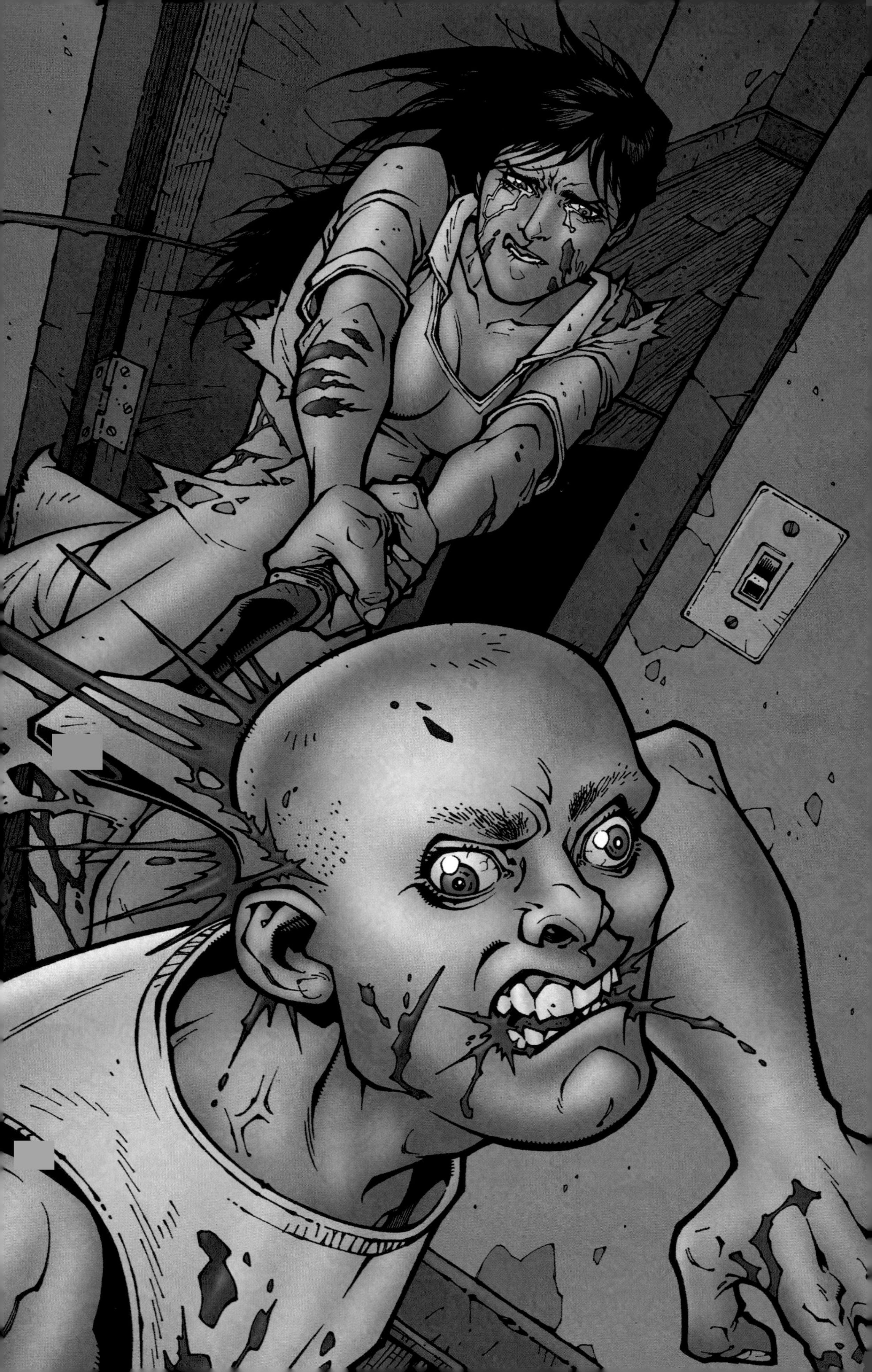

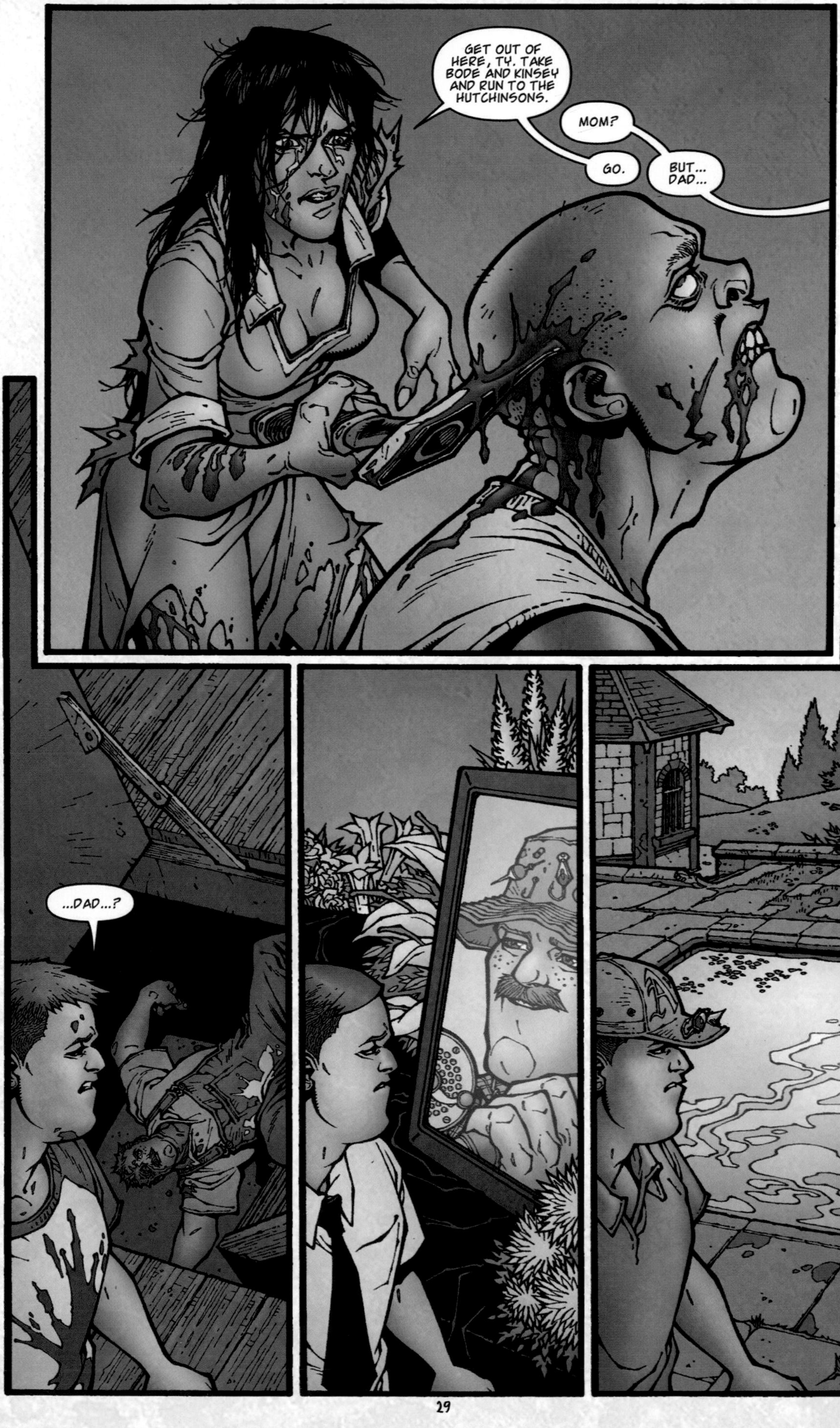
GET OUT OF HERE, TY. TAKE BODE AND KINSEY AND RUN TO THE HUTCHINSONS.
MOM?
GO.
BUT... DAD...
...DAD...?

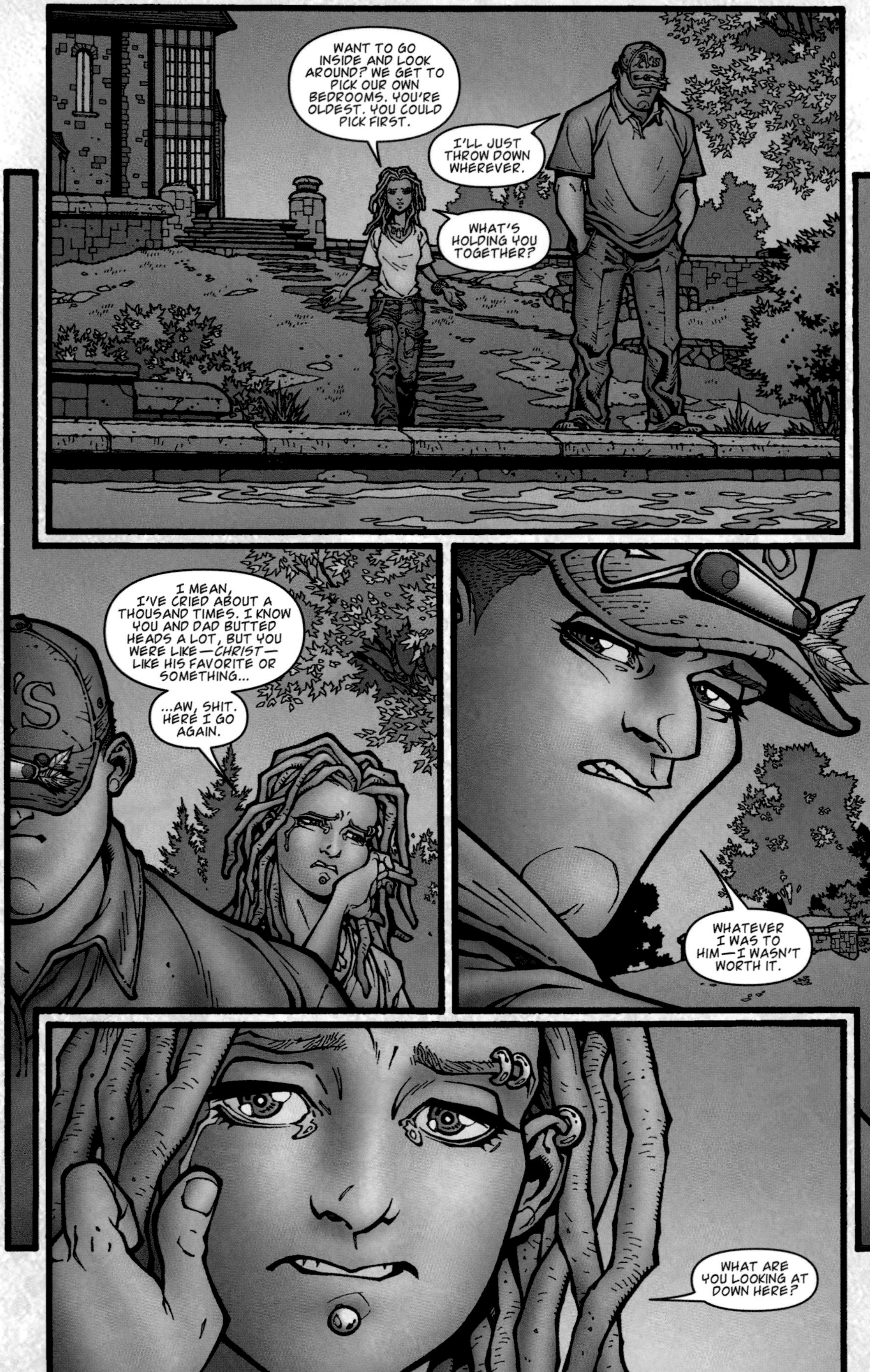
WANT TO GO INSIDE AND LOOK AROUND? WE GET TO PICK OUR OWN BEDROOMS. YOU'RE OLDEST. YOU COULD PICK FIRST.
I'LL JUST THROW DOWN WHEREVER.
WHAT'S HOLDING YOU TOGETHER?
I MEAN, I'VE CRIED ABOUT A THOUSAND TIMES. I KNOW YOU AND DAD BUTTED HEADS A LOT, BUT YOU WERE LIKE—*CHRIST*—LIKE HIS FAVORITE OR SOMETHING...
...AW, SHIT. HERE I GO AGAIN.
WHATEVER I WAS TO HIM—I WASN'T WORTH IT.
WHAT ARE YOU LOOKING AT DOWN HERE?

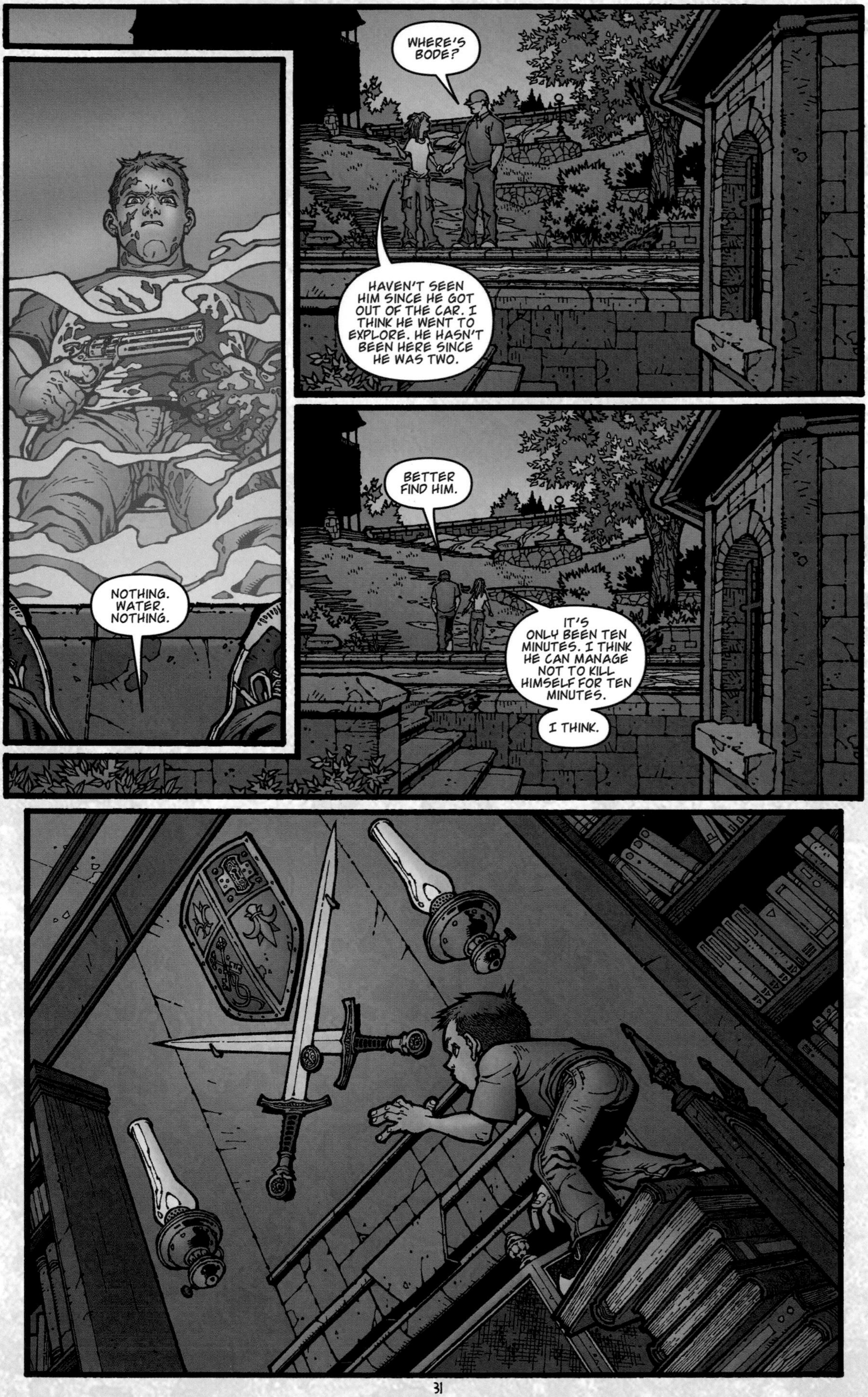
WHERE'S BODE?
HAVEN'T SEEN HIM SINCE HE GOT OUT OF THE CAR. I THINK HE WENT TO EXPLORE. HE HASN'T BEEN HERE SINCE HE WAS TWO.
NOTHING. WATER. NOTHING.
BETTER FIND HIM.
IT'S ONLY BEEN TEN MINUTES. I THINK HE CAN MANAGE NOT TO KILL HIMSELF FOR TEN MINUTES.
I THINK.

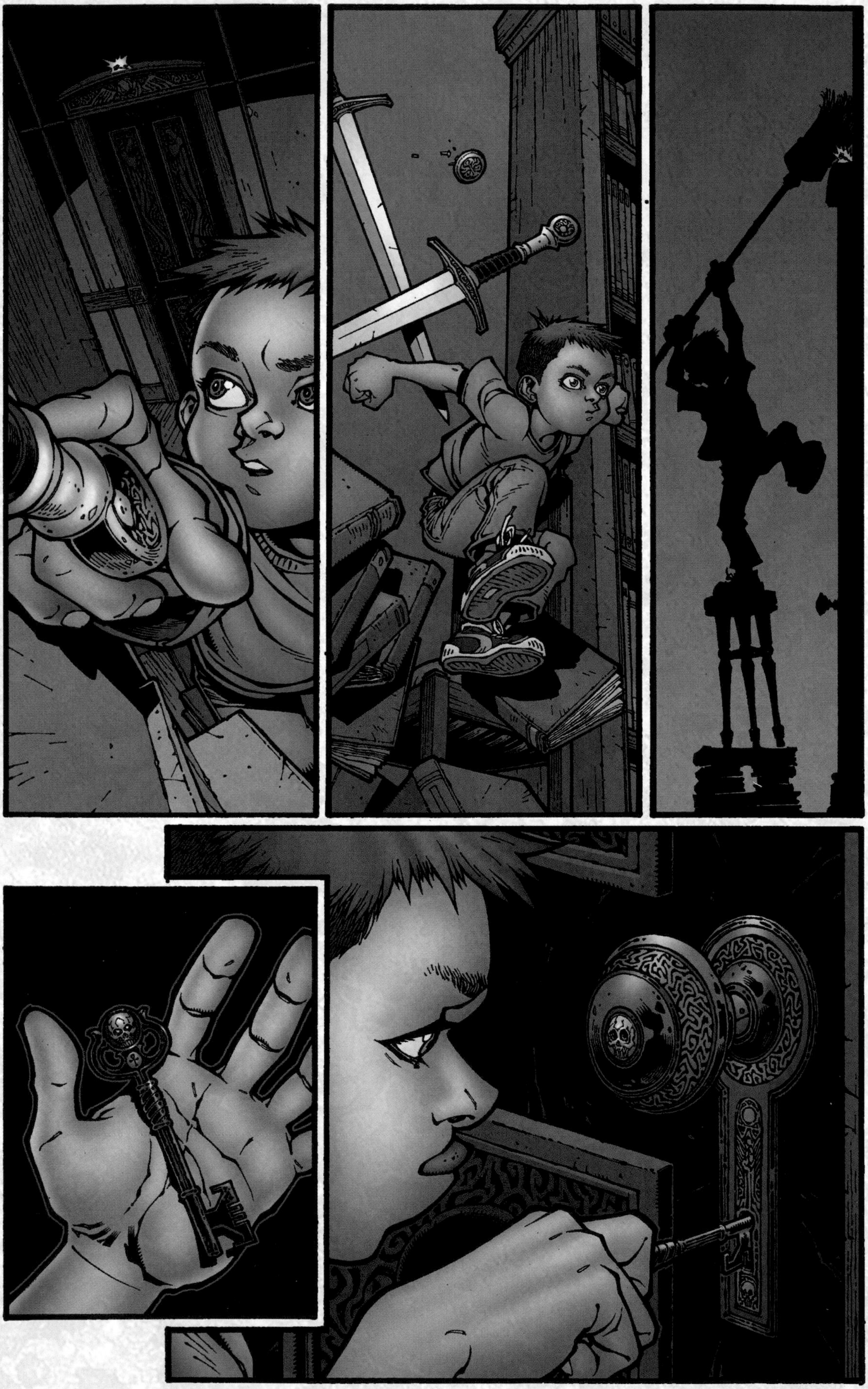

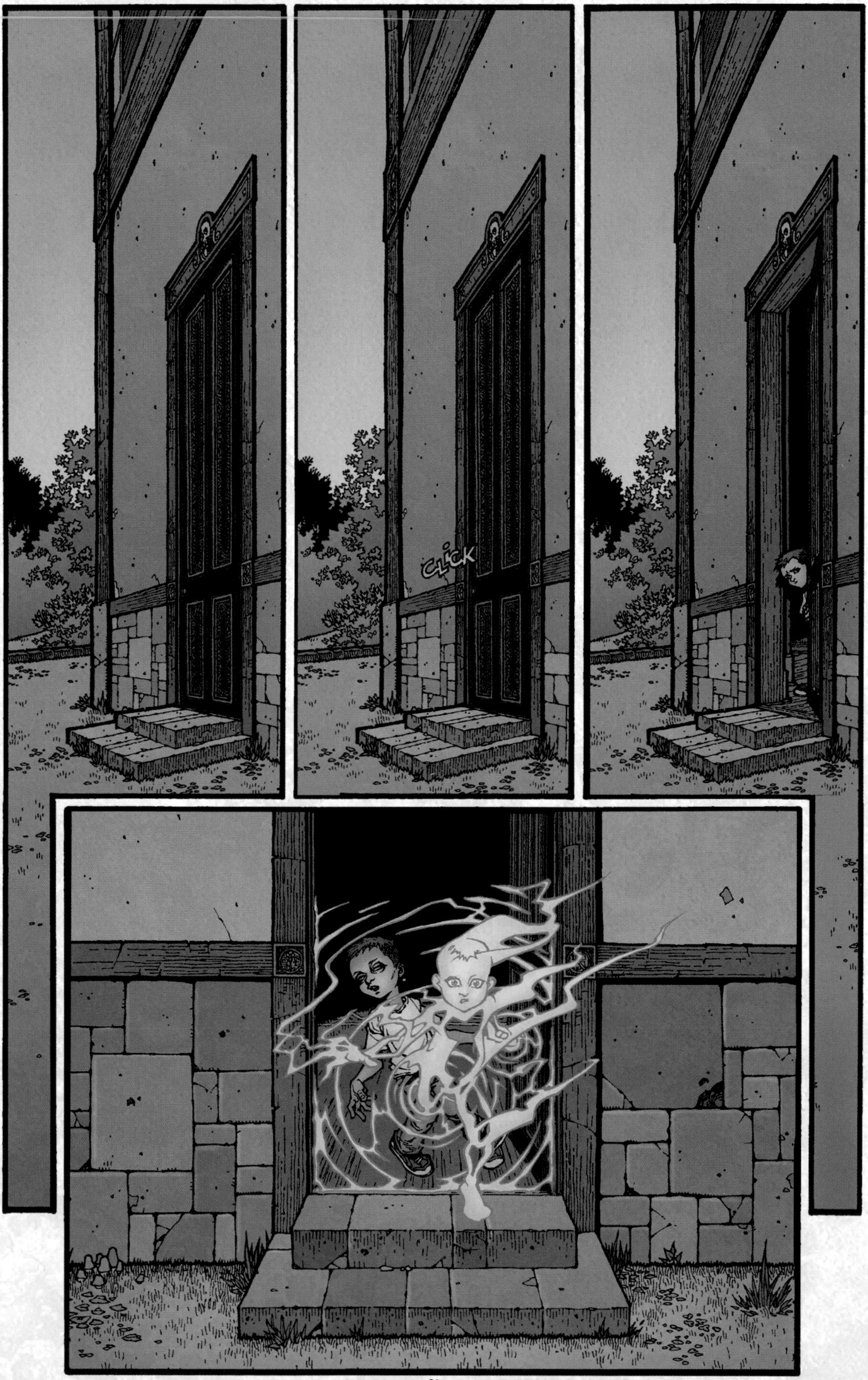
CLICK

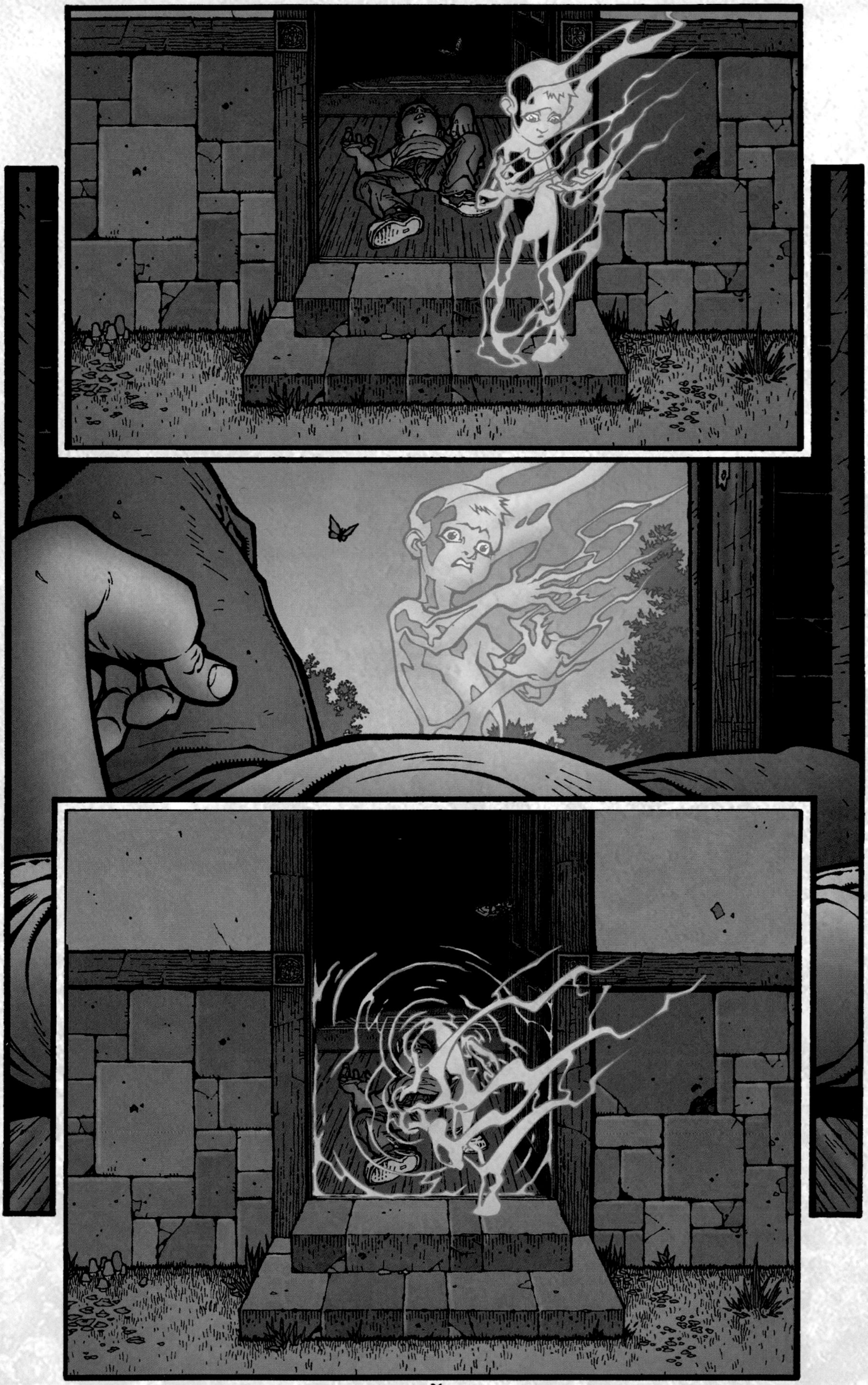

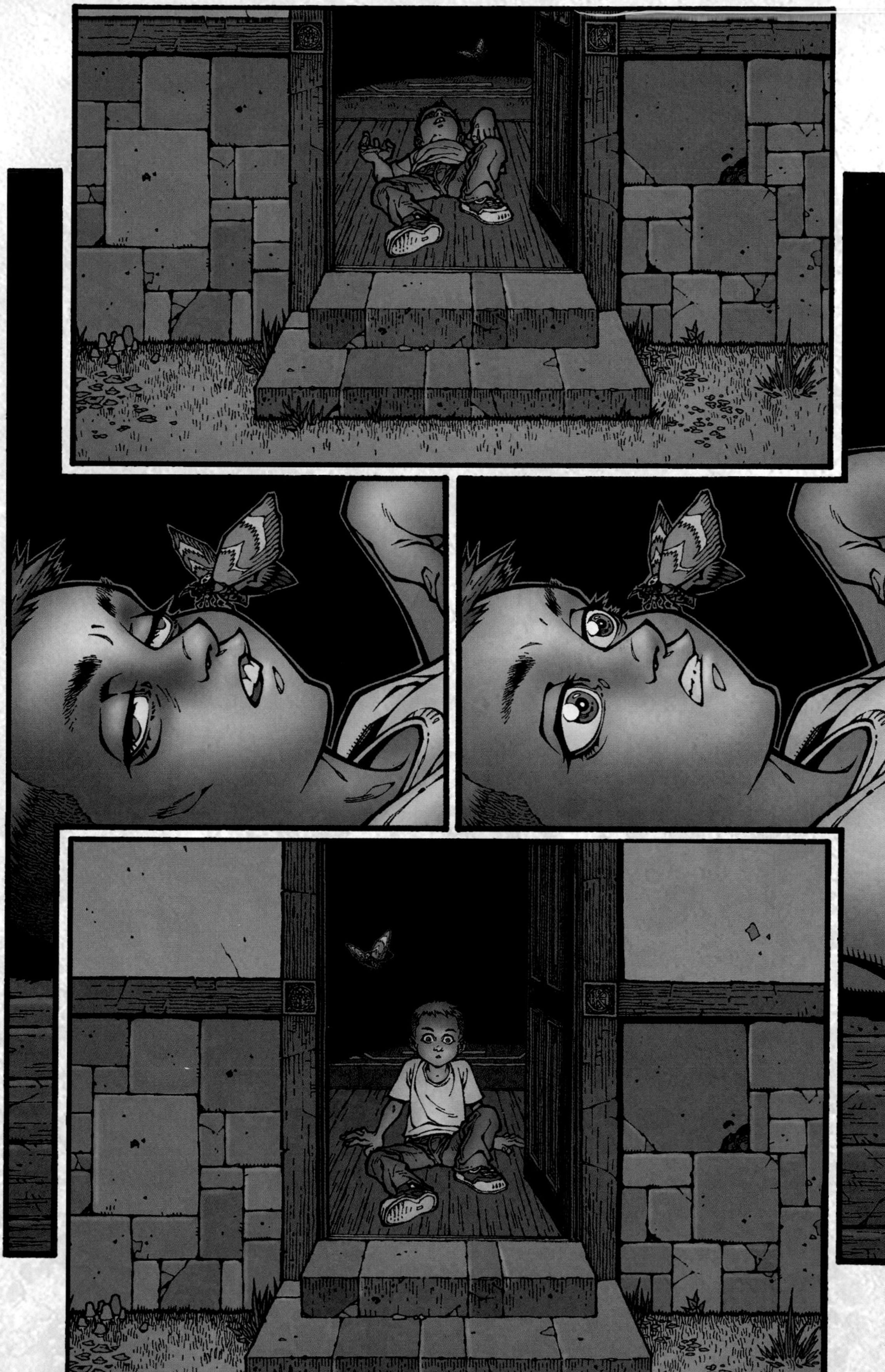

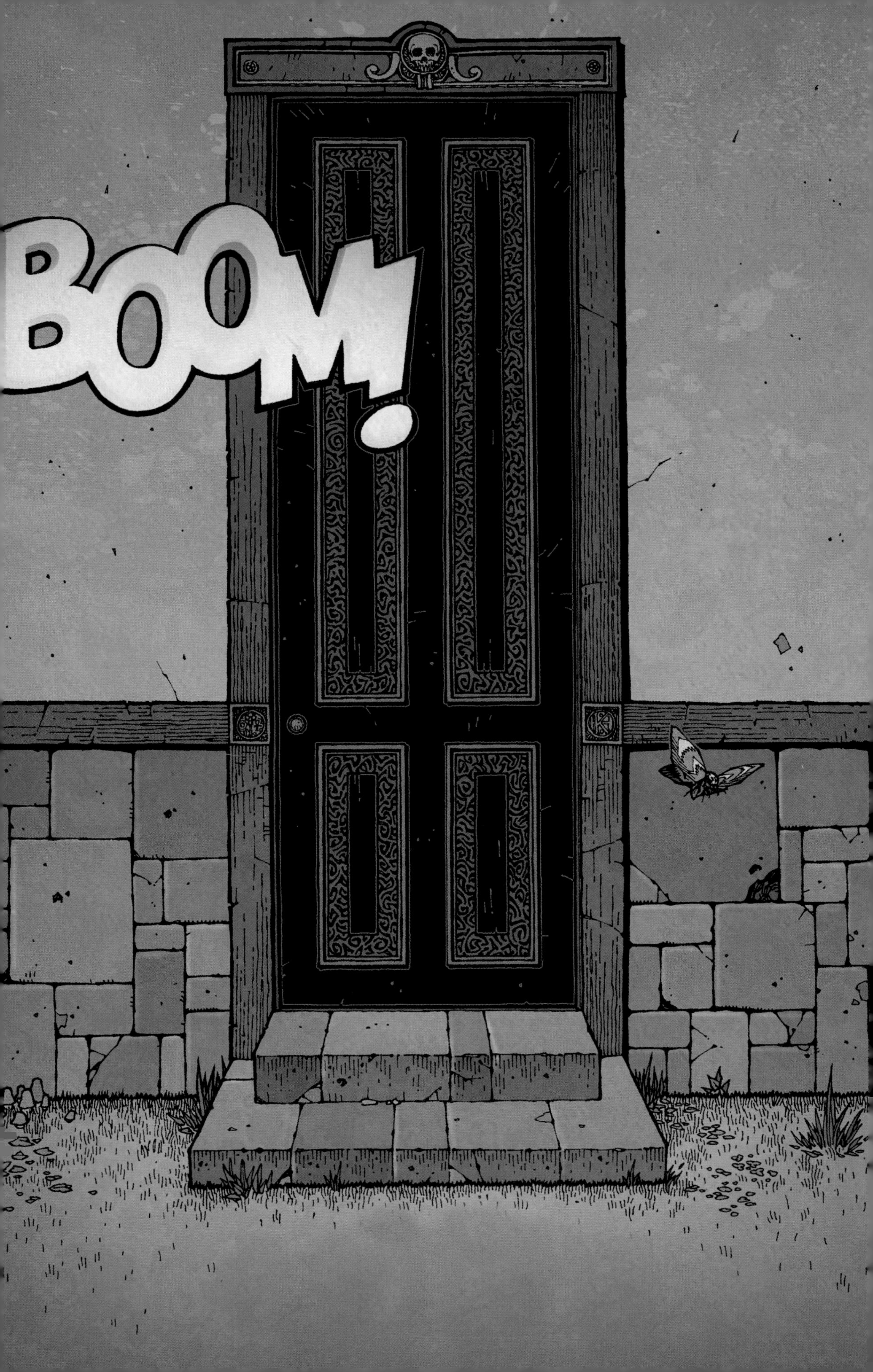
BOOM!

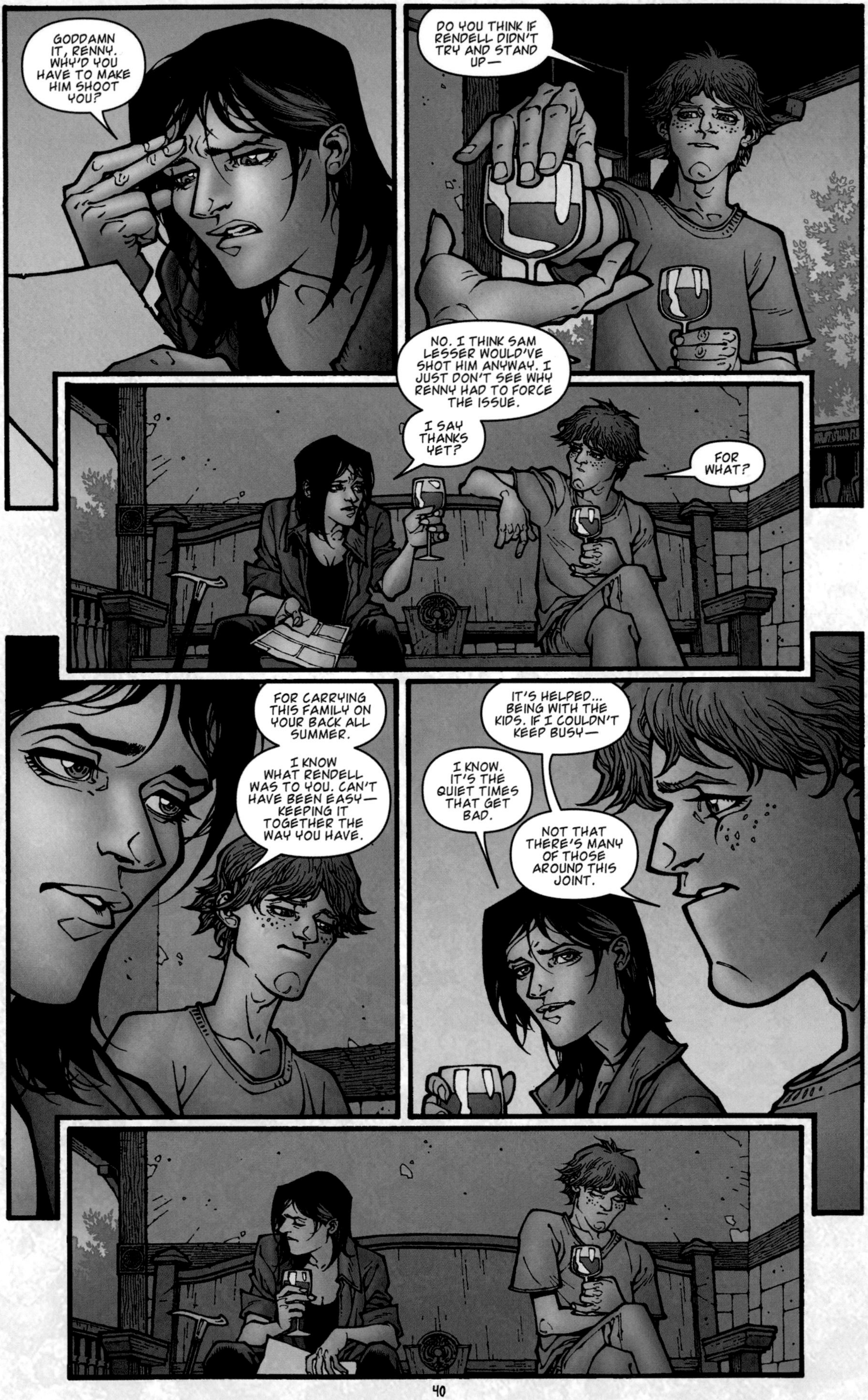
GODDAMN IT, RENNY. WHY'D YOU HAVE TO MAKE HIM SHOOT YOU?
DO YOU THINK IF RENDELL DIDN'T TRY AND STAND UP—
NO. I THINK SAM LESSER WOULD'VE SHOT HIM ANYWAY. I JUST DON'T SEE WHY RENNY HAD TO FORCE THE ISSUE.
I SAY THANKS YET?
FOR WHAT?
FOR CARRYING THIS FAMILY ON YOUR BACK ALL SUMMER.
I KNOW WHAT RENDELL WAS TO YOU. CAN'T HAVE BEEN EASY—KEEPING IT TOGETHER THE WAY YOU HAVE.
IT'S HELPED... BEING WITH THE KIDS. IF I COULDN'T KEEP BUSY—
I KNOW. IT'S THE QUIET TIMES THAT GET BAD.
NOT THAT THERE'S MANY OF THOSE AROUND THIS JOINT.

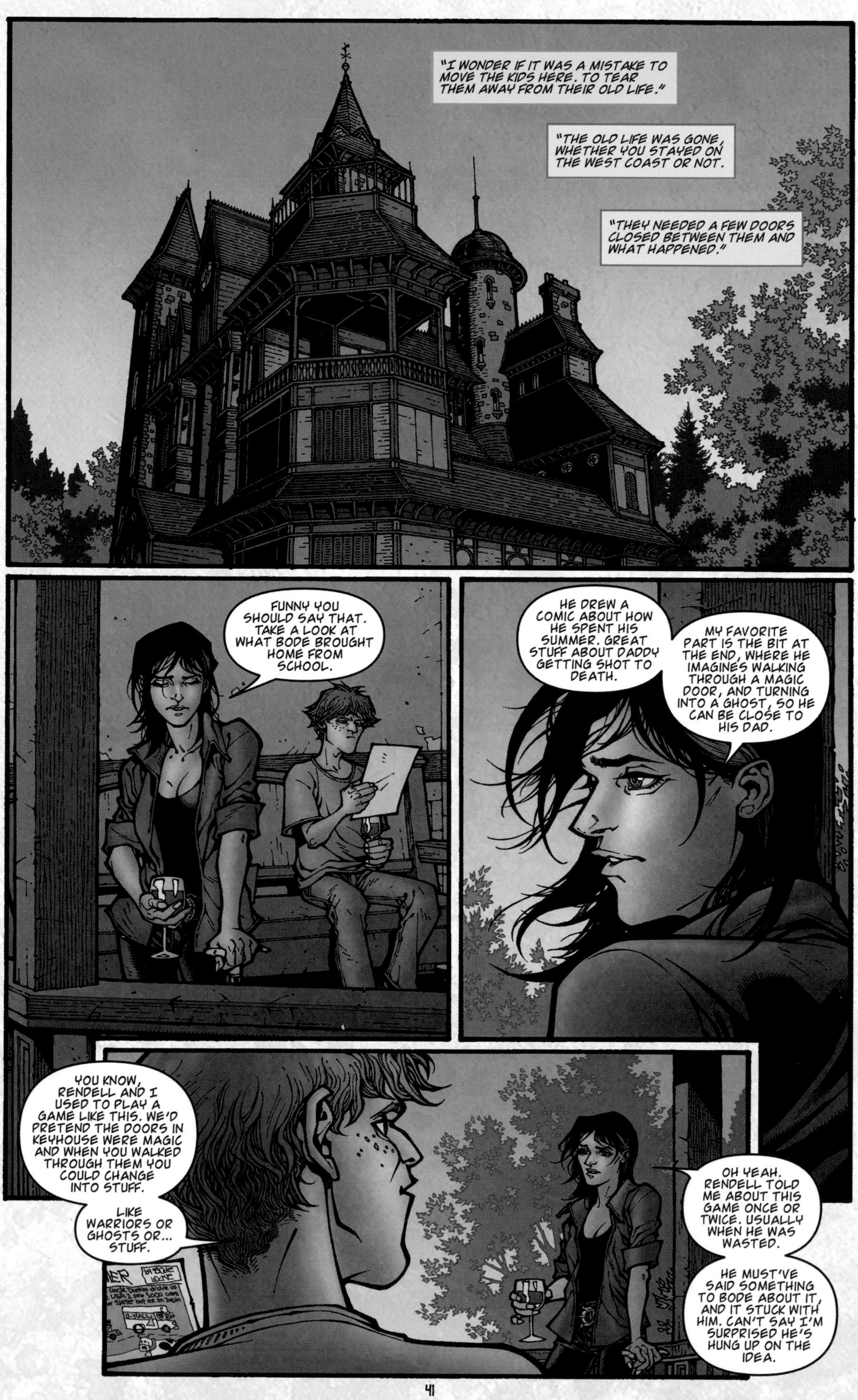
"I WONDER IF IT WAS A MISTAKE TO MOVE THE KIDS HERE. TO TEAR THEM AWAY FROM THEIR OLD LIFE."
"THE OLD LIFE WAS GONE, WHETHER YOU STAYED ON THE WEST COAST OR NOT.
"THEY NEEDED A FEW DOORS CLOSED BETWEEN THEM AND WHAT HAPPENED."
FUNNY YOU SHOULD SAY THAT. TAKE A LOOK AT WHAT BODE BROUGHT HOME FROM SCHOOL.
HE DREW A COMIC ABOUT HOW HE SPENT HIS SUMMER. GREAT STUFF ABOUT DADDY GETTING SHOT TO DEATH.
MY FAVORITE PART IS THE BIT AT THE END, WHERE HE IMAGINES WALKING THROUGH A MAGIC DOOR, AND TURNING INTO A GHOST, SO HE CAN BE CLOSE TO HIS DAD.
YOU KNOW, RENDELL AND I USED TO PLAY A GAME LIKE THIS. WE'D PRETEND THE DOORS IN KEYHOUSE WERE MAGIC AND WHEN YOU WALKED THROUGH THEM YOU COULD CHANGE INTO STUFF.
LIKE WARRIORS OR GHOSTS OR... STUFF.
OH YEAH. RENDELL TOLD ME ABOUT THIS GAME ONCE OR TWICE. USUALLY WHEN HE WAS WASTED.
HE MUST'VE SAID SOMETHING TO BODE ABOUT IT, AND IT STUCK WITH HIM. CAN'T SAY I'M SURPRISED HE'S HUNG UP ON THE IDEA.

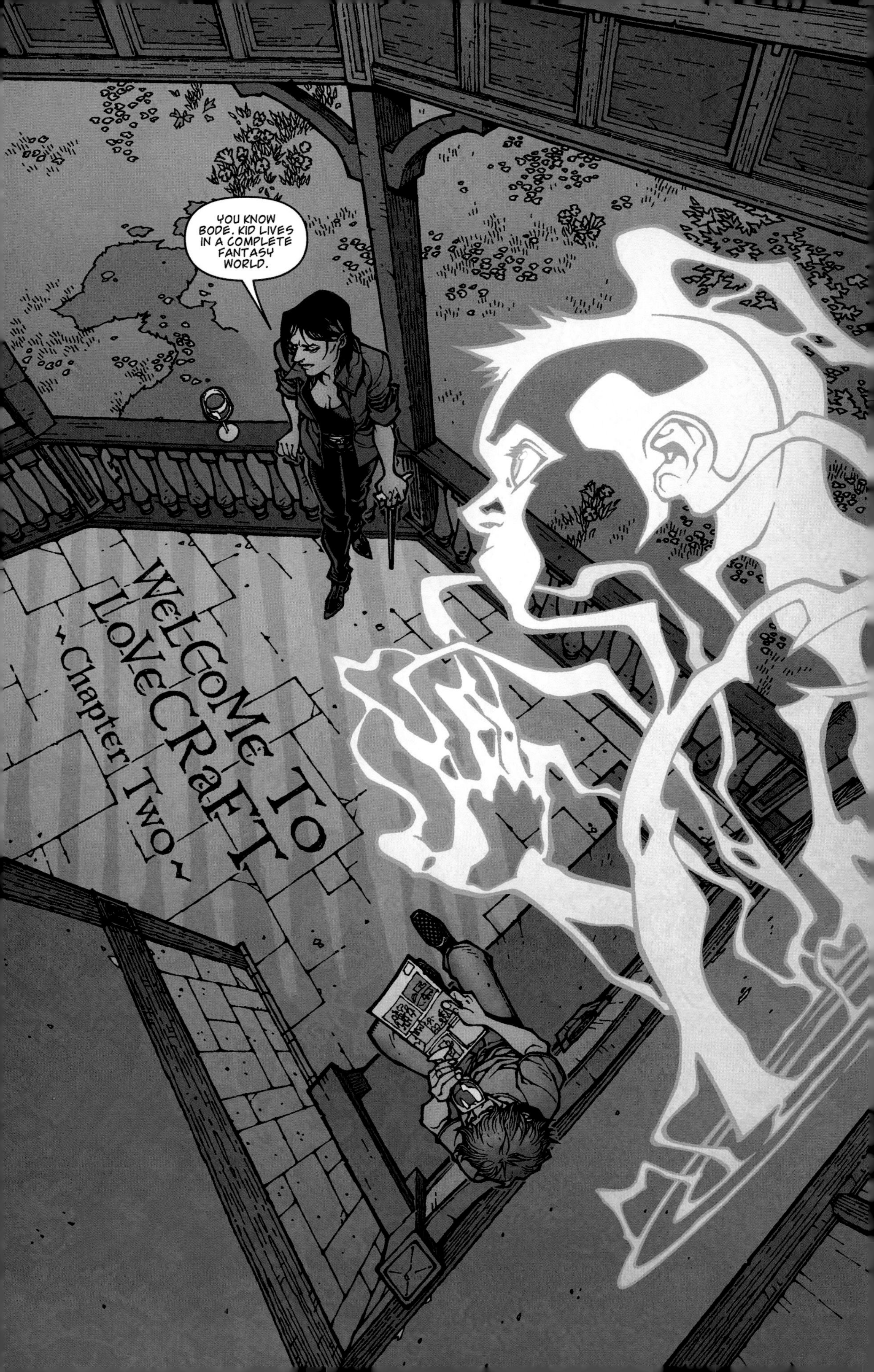
YOU KNOW BODE. KID LIVES IN A COMPLETE FANTASY WORLD.
WELCOME TO LOVECRAFT
~Chapter Two~

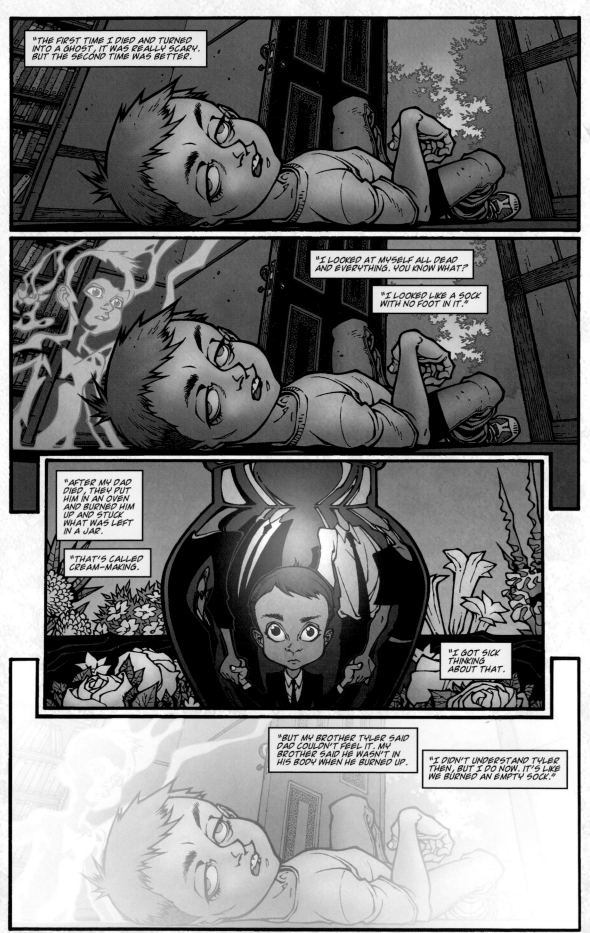

"THE FIRST TIME I DIED AND TURNED INTO A GHOST, IT WAS REALLY SCARY. BUT THE SECOND TIME WAS BETTER.

"I LOOKED AT MYSELF ALL DEAD AND EVERYTHING. YOU KNOW WHAT?

"I LOOKED LIKE A SOCK WITH NO FOOT IN IT."

"AFTER MY DAD DIED, THEY PUT HIM IN AN OVEN AND BURNED HIM UP AND STUCK WHAT WAS LEFT IN A JAR.

"THAT'S CALLED CREAM-MAKING.

"I GOT SICK THINKING ABOUT THAT.

"BUT MY BROTHER TYLER SAID DAD COULDN'T FEEL IT. MY BROTHER SAID HE WASN'T IN HIS BODY WHEN HE BURNED UP.

"I DIDN'T UNDERSTAND TYLER THEN, BUT I DO NOW. IT'S LIKE WE BURNED AN EMPTY SOCK."

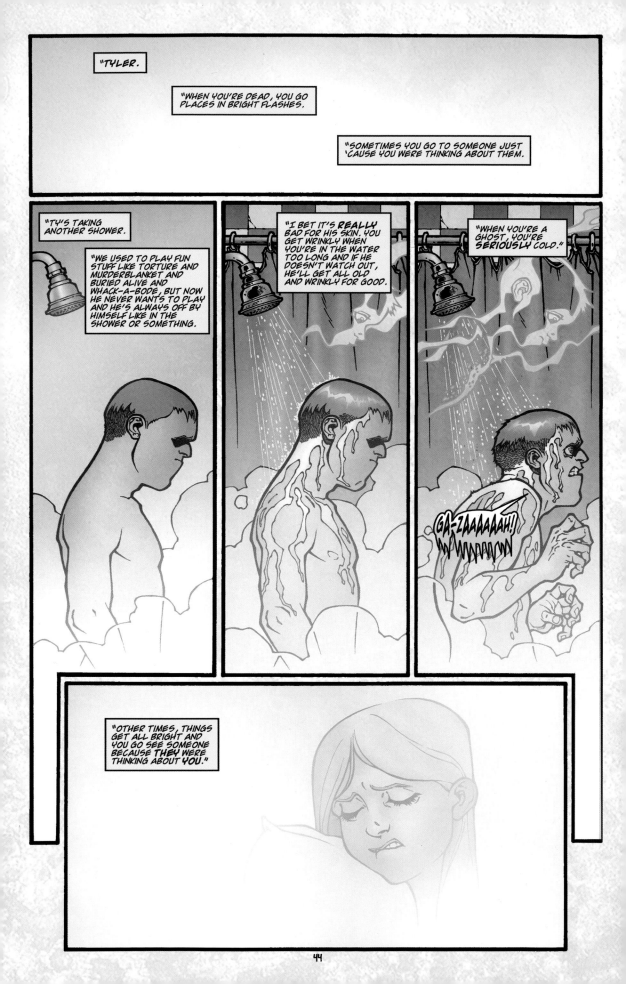

"TYLER.

"WHEN YOU'RE DEAD, YOU GO PLACES IN BRIGHT FLASHES.

"SOMETIMES YOU GO TO SOMEONE JUST 'CAUSE YOU WERE THINKING ABOUT THEM.

"TY'S TAKING ANOTHER SHOWER.

"WE USED TO PLAY FUN STUFF LIKE TORTURE AND MURDERBLANKET AND BURIED ALIVE AND WHACK-A-BODE, BUT NOW HE NEVER WANTS TO PLAY AND HE'S ALWAYS OFF BY HIMSELF LIKE IN THE SHOWER OR SOMETHING.

"I BET IT'S REALLY BAD FOR HIS SKIN. YOU GET WRINKLY WHEN YOU'RE IN THE WATER TOO LONG AND IF HE DOESN'T WATCH OUT, HE'LL GET ALL OLD AND WRINKLY FOR GOOD.

"WHEN YOU'RE A GHOST, YOU'RE SERIOUSLY COLD."

GA-ZAAAAAAH!

"OTHER TIMES, THINGS GET ALL BRIGHT AND YOU GO SEE SOMEONE BECAUSE THEY WERE THINKING ABOUT YOU."

44

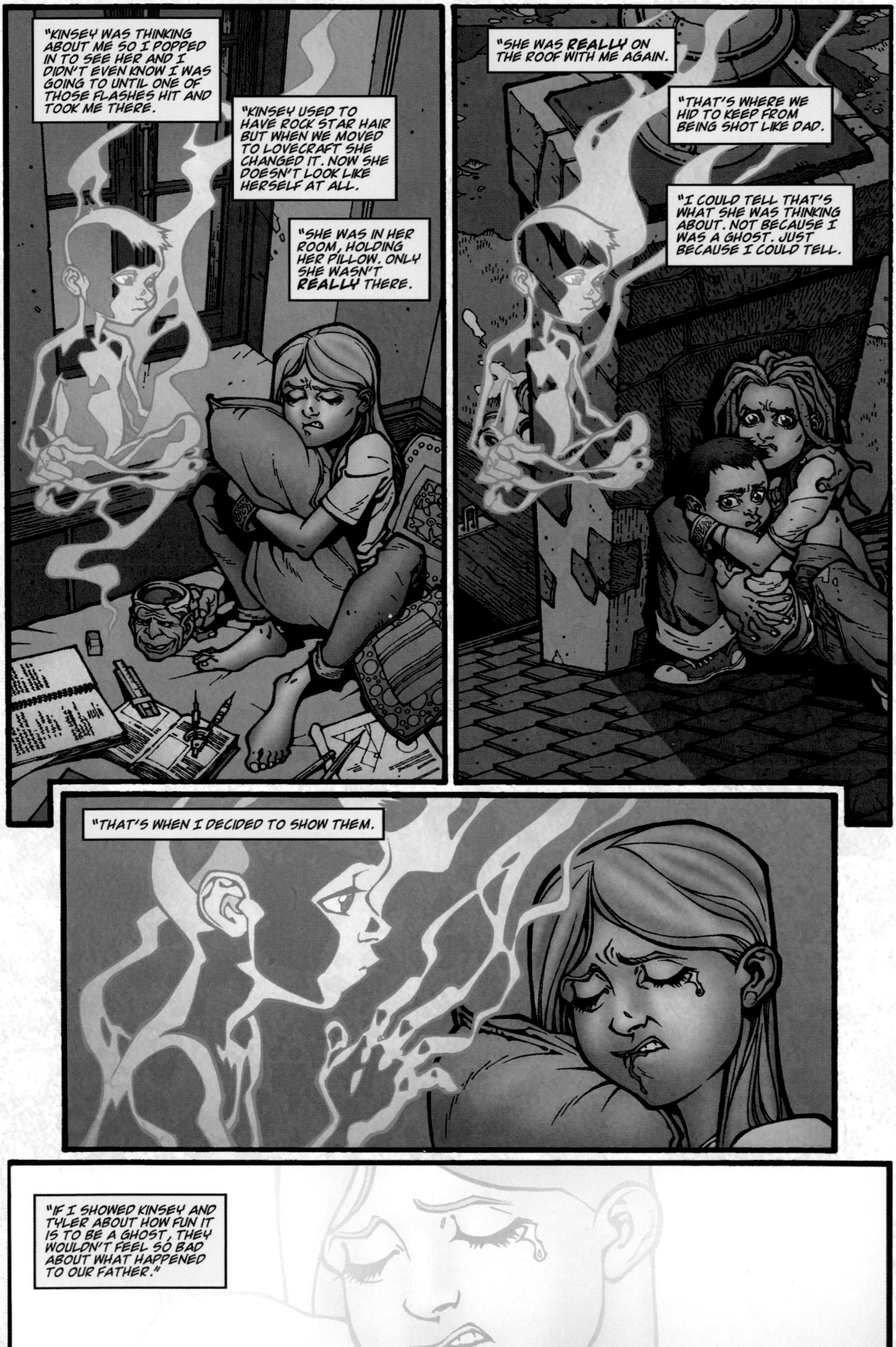
"KINSEY WAS THINKING ABOUT ME SO I POPPED IN TO SEE HER AND I DIDN'T EVEN KNOW I WAS GOING TO UNTIL ONE OF THOSE FLASHES HIT AND TOOK ME THERE.
"KINSEY USED TO HAVE ROCK STAR HAIR BUT WHEN WE MOVED TO LOVECRAFT SHE CHANGED IT. NOW SHE DOESN'T LOOK LIKE HERSELF AT ALL.
"SHE WAS IN HER ROOM, HOLDING HER PILLOW. ONLY SHE WASN'T REALLY THERE.
"SHE WAS REALLY ON THE ROOF WITH ME AGAIN.
"THAT'S WHERE WE HID TO KEEP FROM BEING SHOT LIKE DAD.
"I COULD TELL THAT'S WHAT SHE WAS THINKING ABOUT. NOT BECAUSE I WAS A GHOST. JUST BECAUSE I COULD TELL.
"THAT'S WHEN I DECIDED TO SHOW THEM.
"IF I SHOWED KINSEY AND TYLER ABOUT HOW FUN IT IS TO BE A GHOST, THEY WOULDN'T FEEL SO BAD ABOUT WHAT HAPPENED TO OUR FATHER."

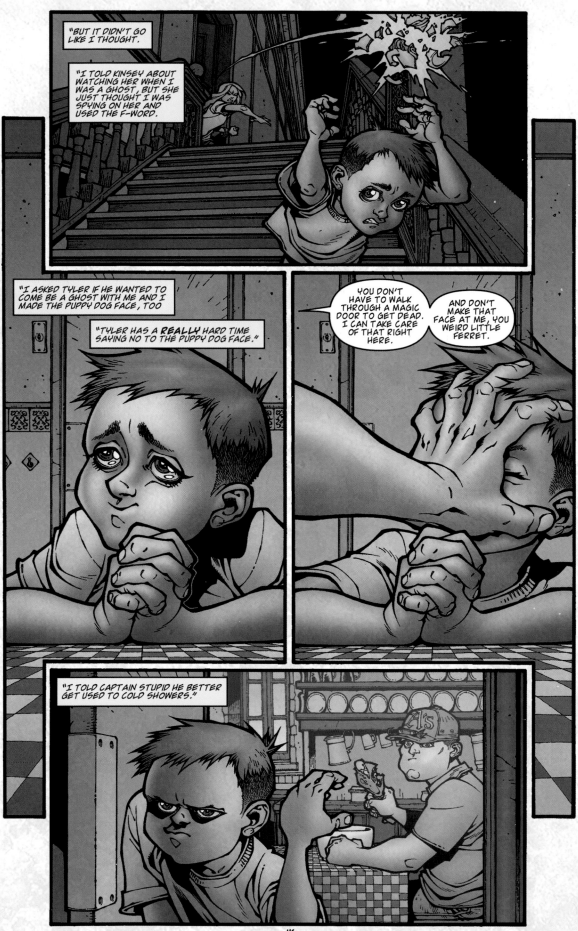

"BUT IT DIDN'T GO LIKE I THOUGHT.

"I TOLD KINSEY ABOUT WATCHING HER WHEN I WAS A GHOST, BUT SHE JUST THOUGHT I WAS SPYING ON HER AND USED THE F-WORD.

"I ASKED TYLER IF HE WANTED TO COME BE A GHOST WITH ME AND I MADE THE PUPPY DOG FACE, TOO

"TYLER HAS A **REALLY** HARD TIME SAYING NO TO THE PUPPY DOG FACE."

YOU DON'T HAVE TO WALK THROUGH A MAGIC DOOR TO GET DEAD. I CAN TAKE CARE OF THAT RIGHT HERE.

AND DON'T MAKE THAT FACE AT ME, YOU WEIRD LITTLE FERRET.

"I TOLD CAPTAIN STUPID HE BETTER GET USED TO COLD SHOWERS."

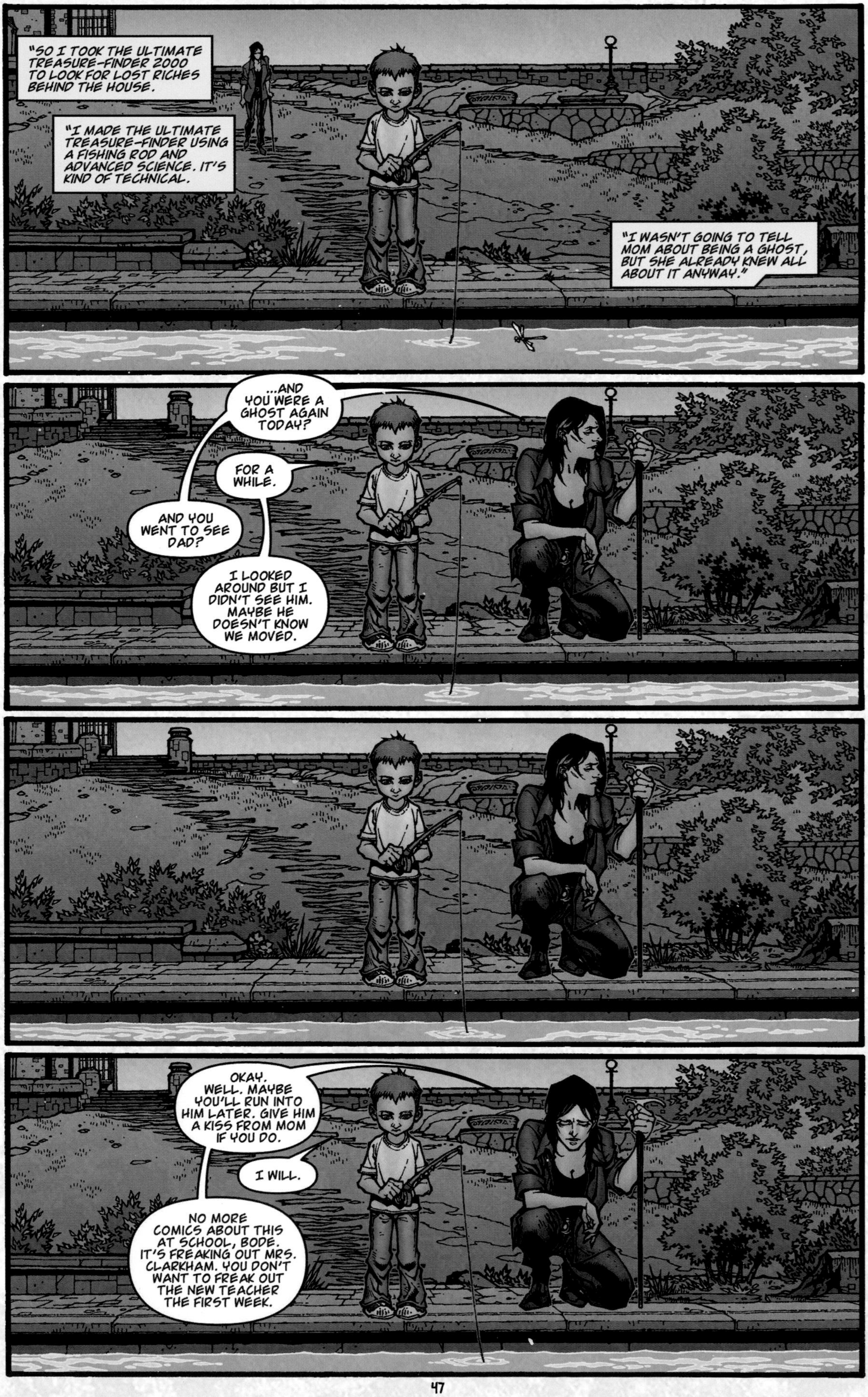
"SO I TOOK THE ULTIMATE TREASURE-FINDER 2000 TO LOOK FOR LOST RICHES BEHIND THE HOUSE.
"I MADE THE ULTIMATE TREASURE-FINDER USING A FISHING ROD AND ADVANCED SCIENCE. IT'S KIND OF TECHNICAL.
"I WASN'T GOING TO TELL MOM ABOUT BEING A GHOST, BUT SHE ALREADY KNEW ALL ABOUT IT ANYWAY."
...AND YOU WERE A GHOST AGAIN TODAY?
FOR A WHILE.
AND YOU WENT TO SEE DAD?
I LOOKED AROUND BUT I DIDN'T SEE HIM. MAYBE HE DOESN'T KNOW WE MOVED.
OKAY. WELL. MAYBE YOU'LL RUN INTO HIM LATER. GIVE HIM A KISS FROM MOM IF YOU DO.
I WILL.
NO MORE COMICS ABOUT THIS AT SCHOOL, BODE. IT'S FREAKING OUT MRS. CLARKHAM. YOU DON'T WANT TO FREAK OUT THE NEW TEACHER THE FIRST WEEK.

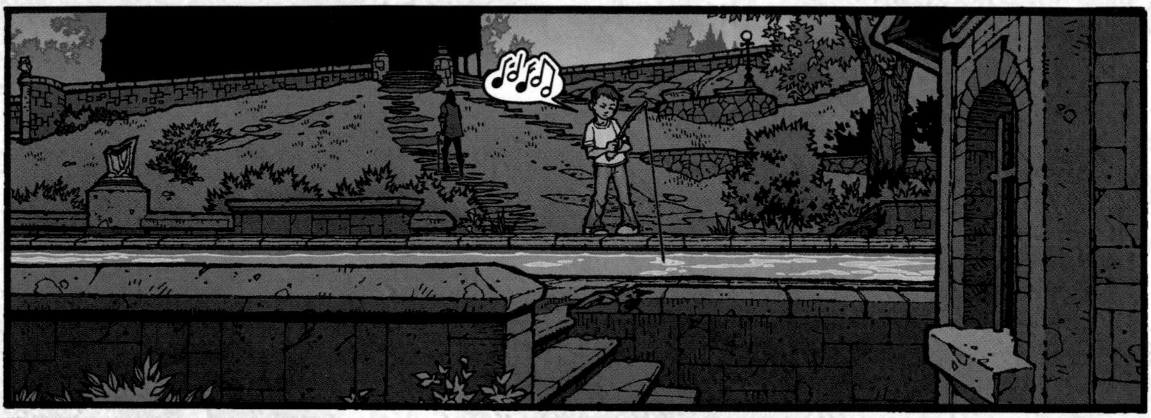

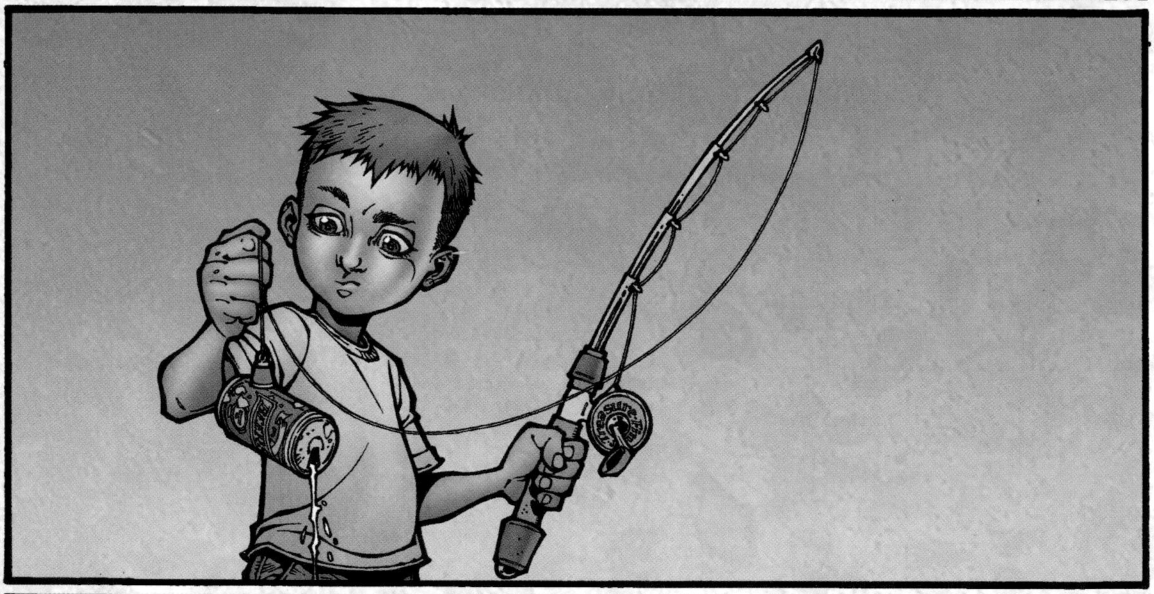

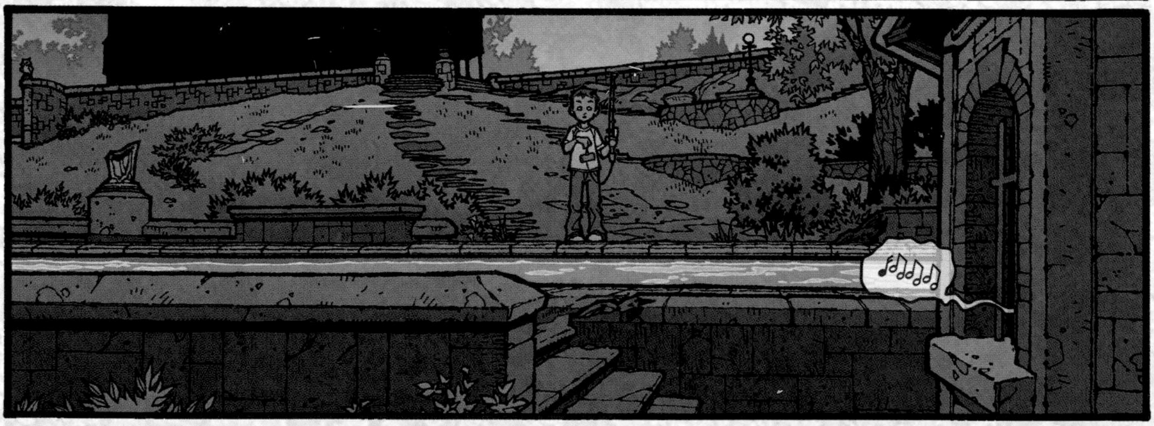

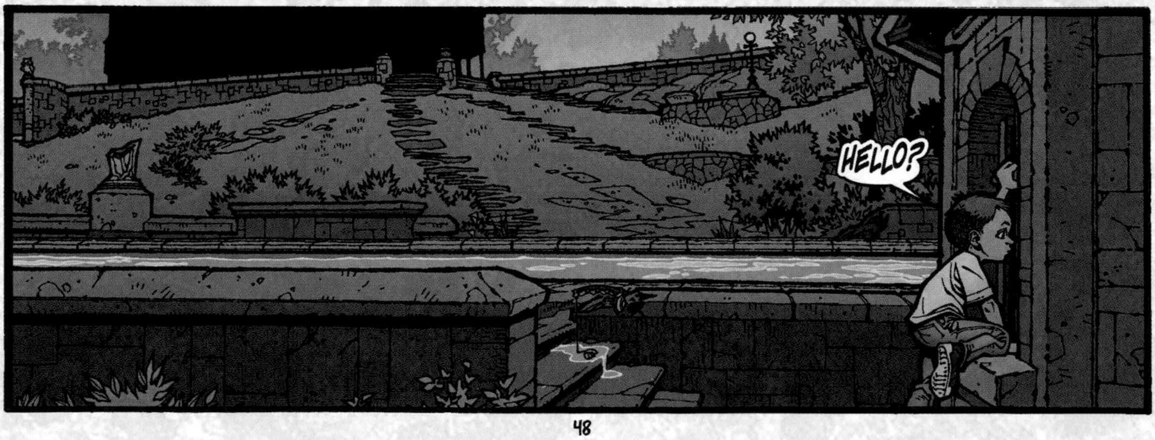
HELLO?

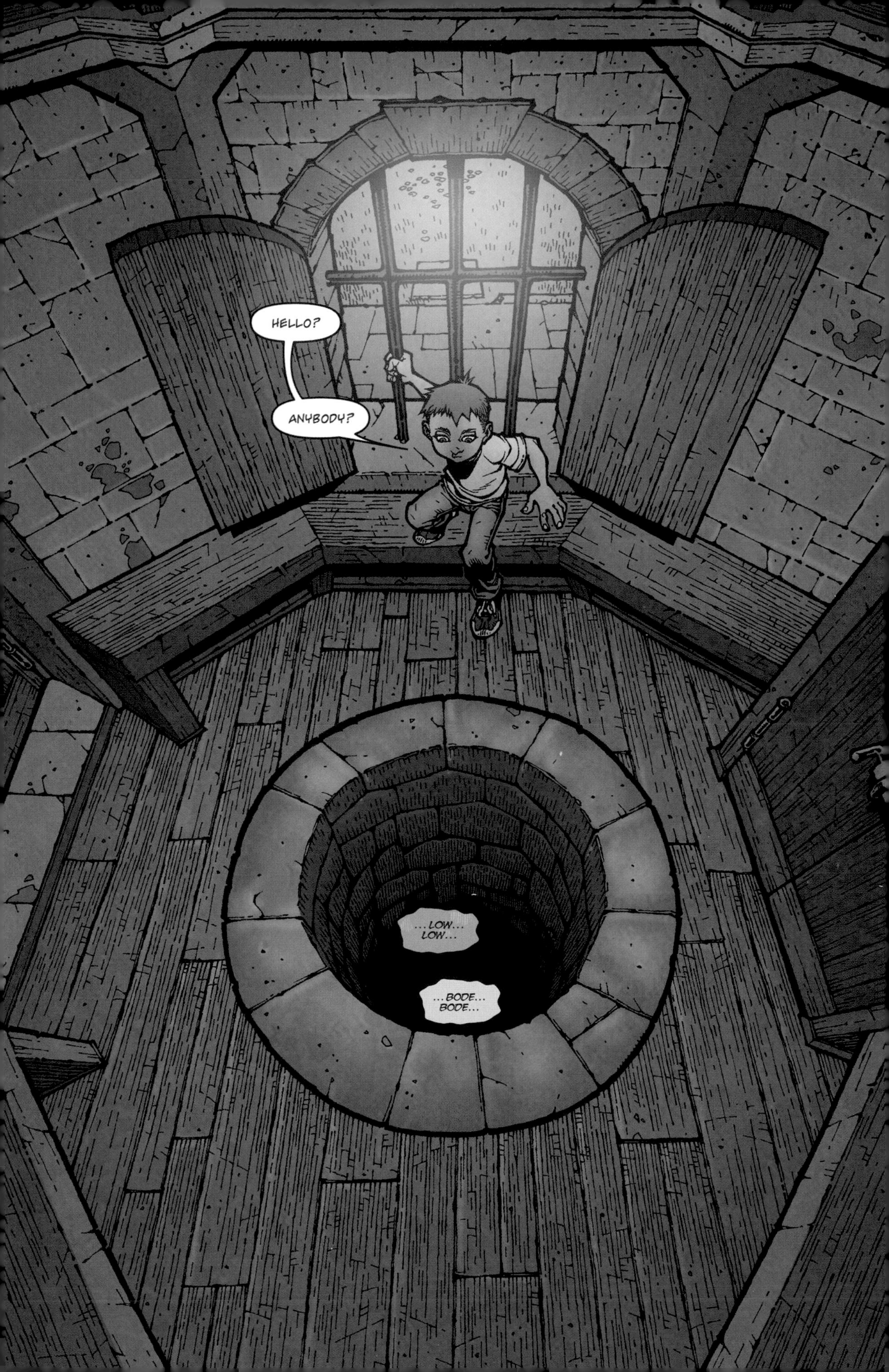
HELLO?
ANYBODY?
...LOW... LOW...
...BODE... BODE...

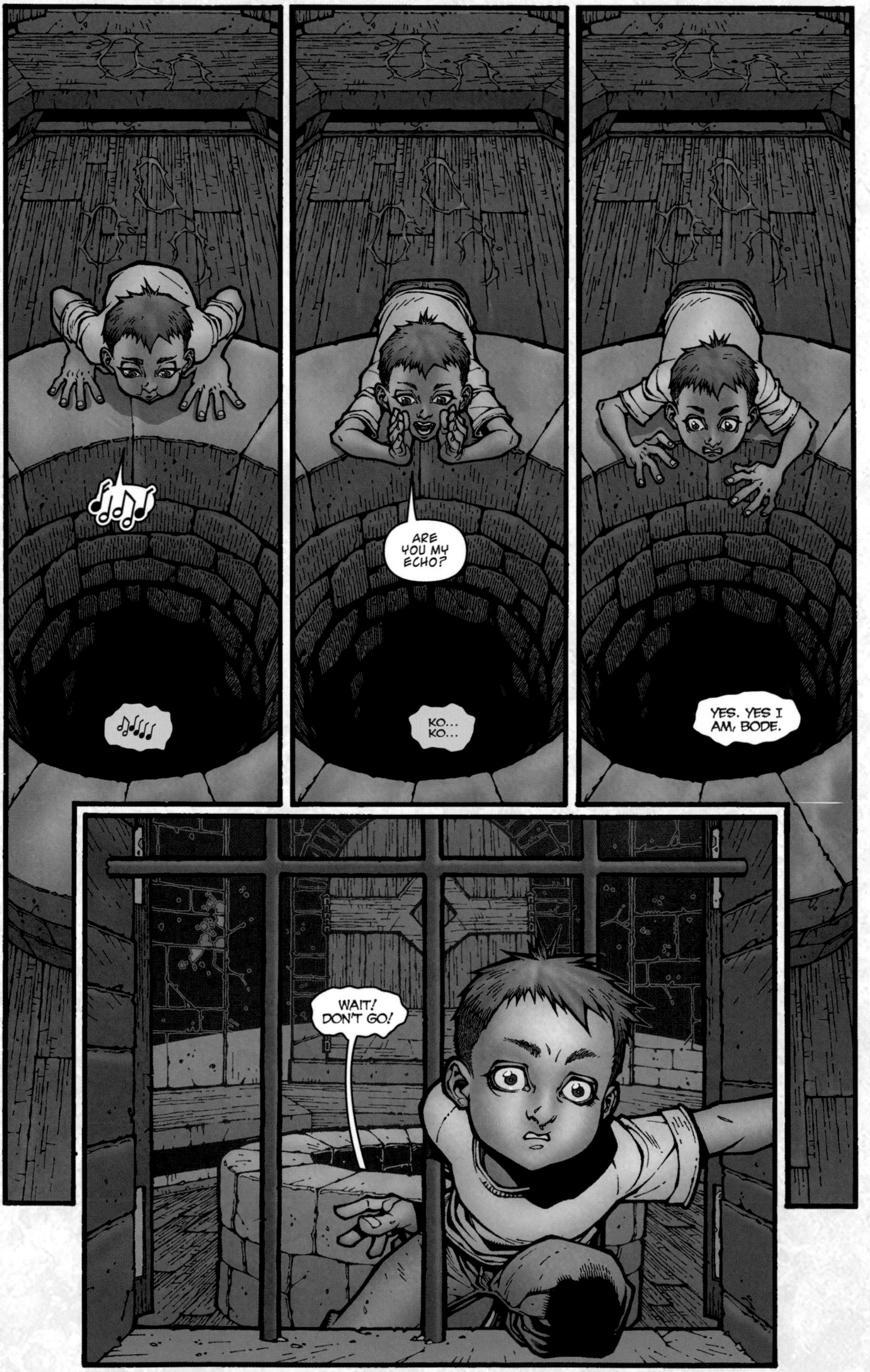
♪♪♪
♪♪♪♪
ARE YOU MY ECHO?
KO... KO...
YES. YES I AM, BODE.
WAIT! DON'T GO!

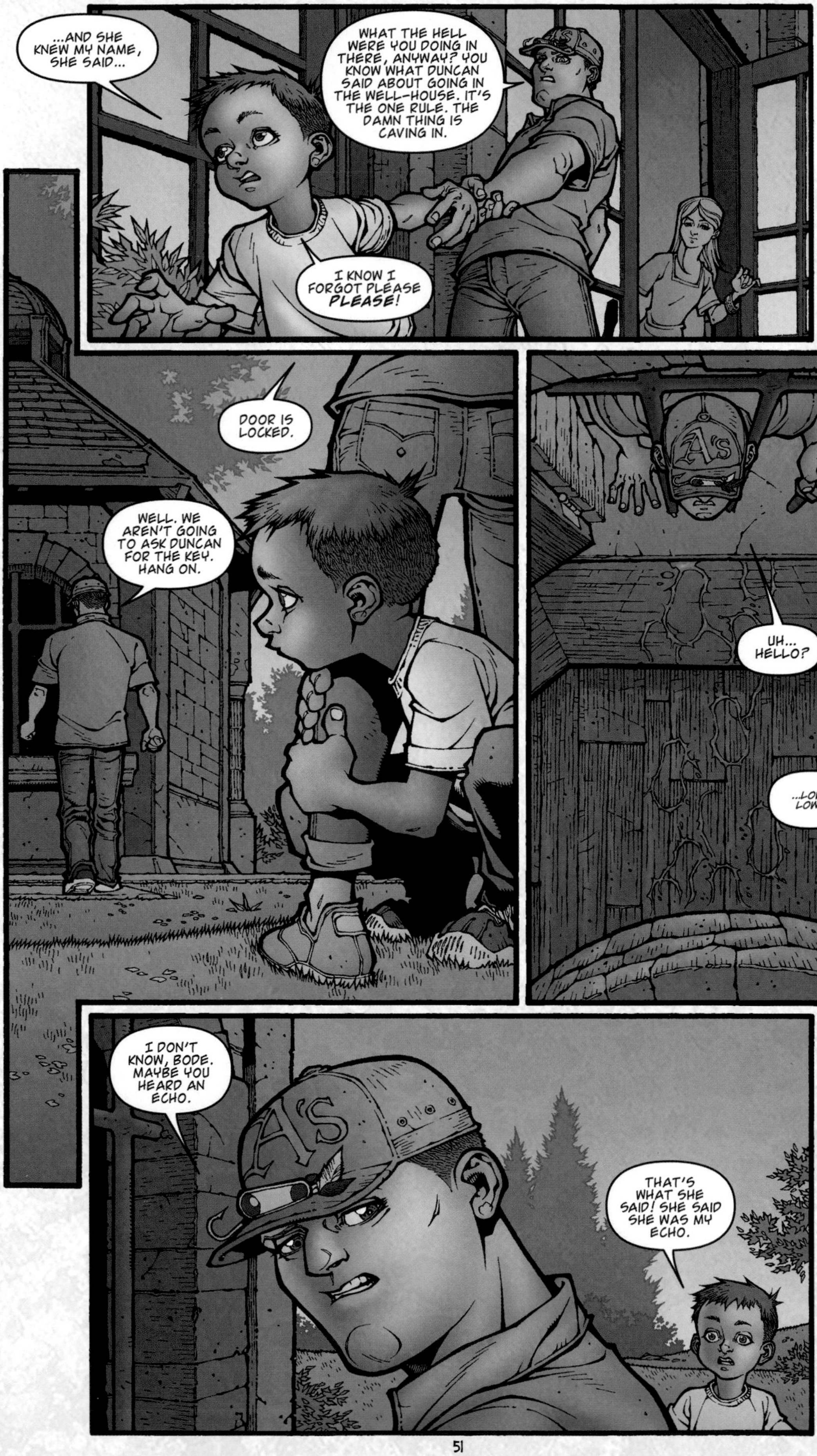
...AND SHE KNEW MY NAME, SHE SAID...
WHAT THE HELL WERE YOU DOING IN THERE, ANYWAY? YOU KNOW WHAT DUNCAN SAID ABOUT GOING IN THE WELL-HOUSE. IT'S THE ONE RULE. THE DAMN THING IS CAVING IN.
I KNOW I FORGOT PLEASE PLEASE!
DOOR IS LOCKED.
WELL. WE AREN'T GOING TO ASK DUNCAN FOR THE KEY. HANG ON.
UH... HELLO?
...LOW... LOW...
I DON'T KNOW, BODE. MAYBE YOU HEARD AN ECHO.
THAT'S WHAT SHE SAID! SHE SAID SHE WAS MY ECHO.

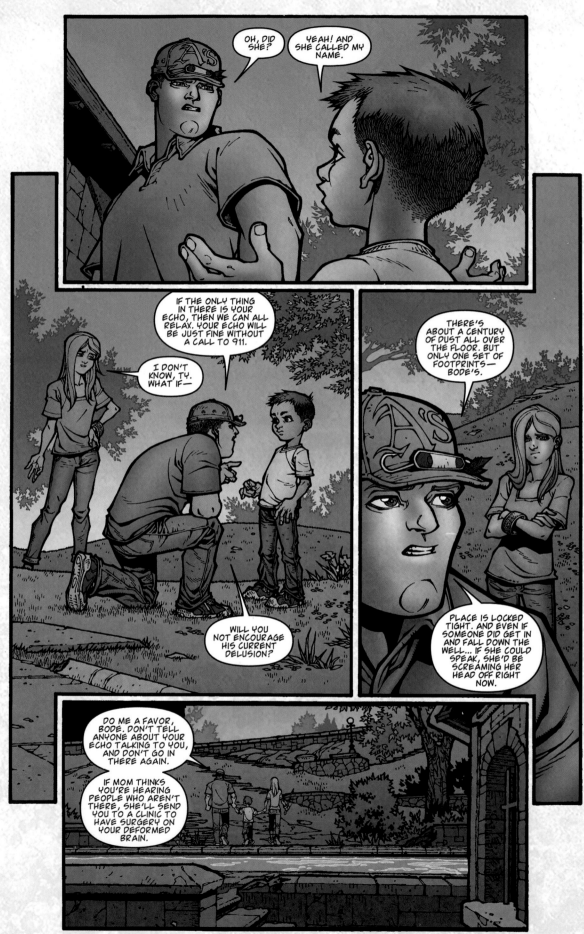

OH, DID SHE?

YEAH! AND SHE CALLED MY NAME.

IF THE ONLY THING IN THERE IS YOUR ECHO, THEN WE CAN ALL RELAX. YOUR ECHO WILL BE JUST FINE WITHOUT A CALL TO 911.

I DON'T KNOW, TY. WHAT IF—

WILL YOU NOT ENCOURAGE HIS CURRENT DELUSION?

THERE'S ABOUT A CENTURY OF DUST ALL OVER THE FLOOR. BUT ONLY ONE SET OF FOOTPRINTS— BODE'S.

PLACE IS LOCKED TIGHT. AND EVEN IF SOMEONE DID GET IN AND FALL DOWN THE WELL... IF SHE COULD SPEAK, SHE'D BE SCREAMING HER HEAD OFF RIGHT NOW.

DO ME A FAVOR, BODE. DON'T TELL ANYONE ABOUT YOUR ECHO TALKING TO YOU, AND DON'T GO IN THERE AGAIN.

IF MOM THINKS YOU'RE HEARING PEOPLE WHO AREN'T THERE, SHE'LL SEND YOU TO A CLINIC TO HAVE SURGERY ON YOUR DEFORMED BRAIN.

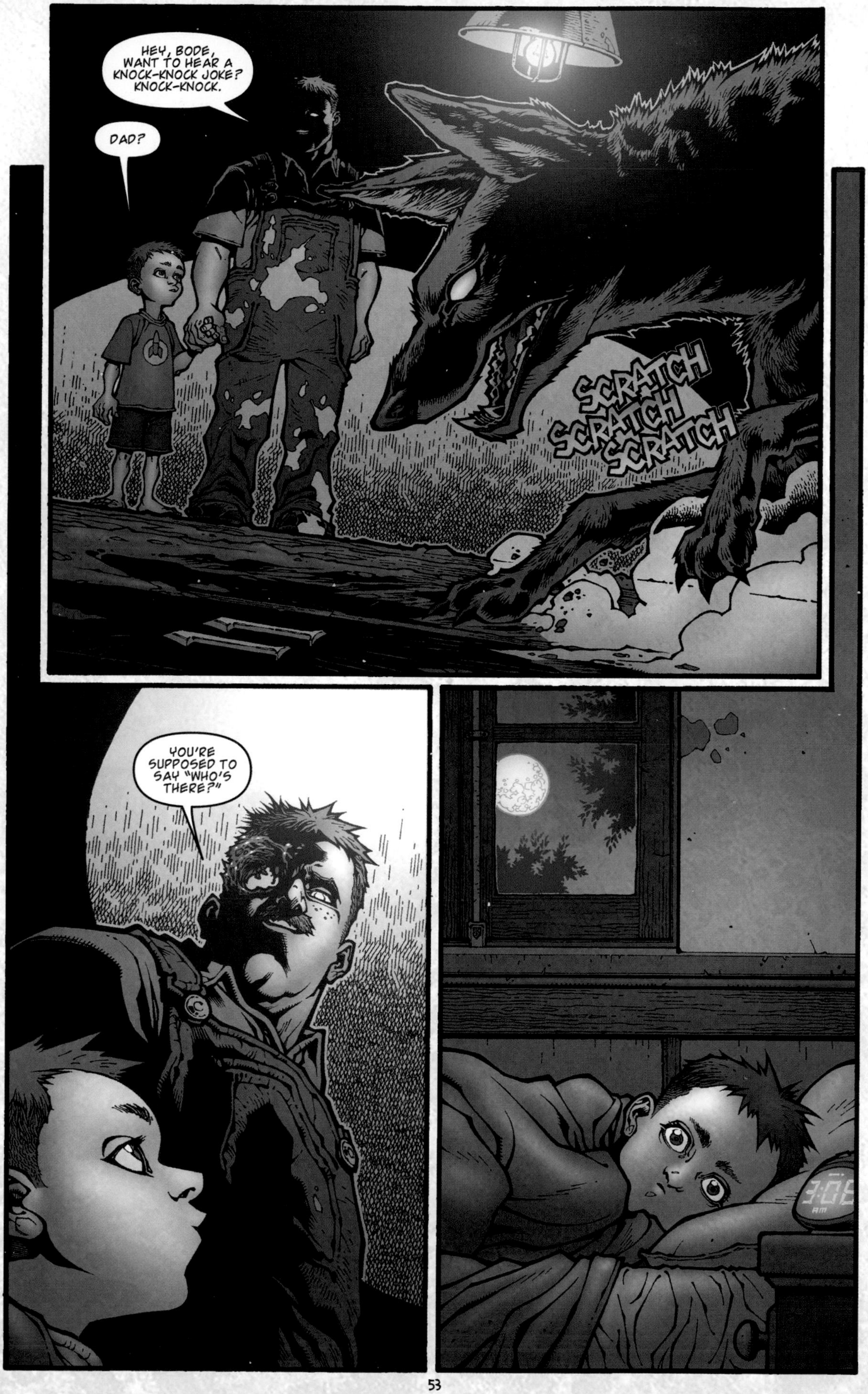
HEY, BODE, WANT TO HEAR A KNOCK-KNOCK JOKE? KNOCK-KNOCK.
DAD?
SCRATCH SCRATCH SCRATCH
YOU'RE SUPPOSED TO SAY "WHO'S THERE?"

54

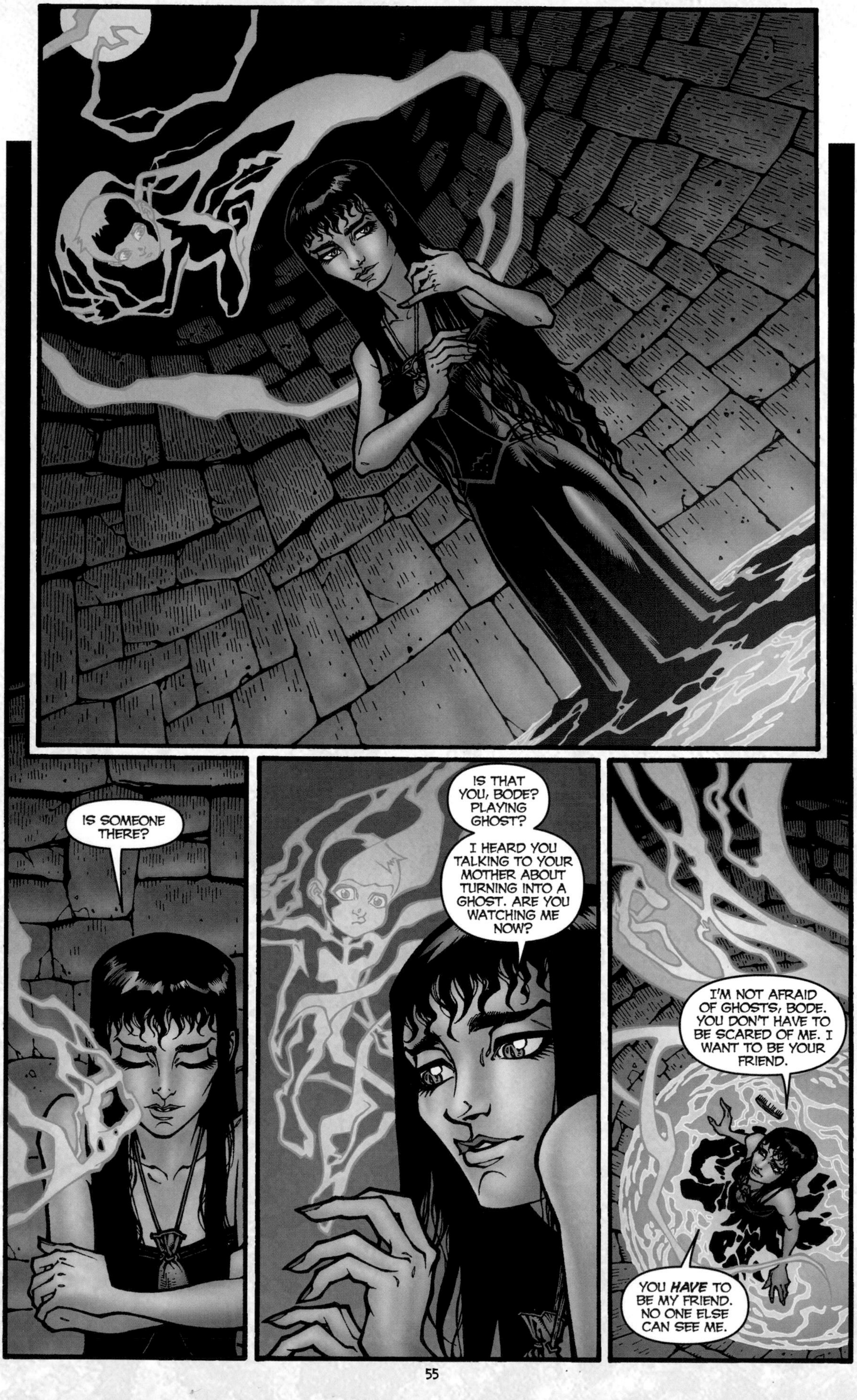
IS SOMEONE THERE?
IS THAT YOU, BODE? PLAYING GHOST?
I HEARD YOU TALKING TO YOUR MOTHER ABOUT TURNING INTO A GHOST. ARE YOU WATCHING ME NOW?
I'M NOT AFRAID OF GHOSTS, BODE. YOU DON'T HAVE TO BE SCARED OF ME. I WANT TO BE YOUR FRIEND.
YOU *HAVE* TO BE MY FRIEND. NO ONE ELSE CAN SEE ME.

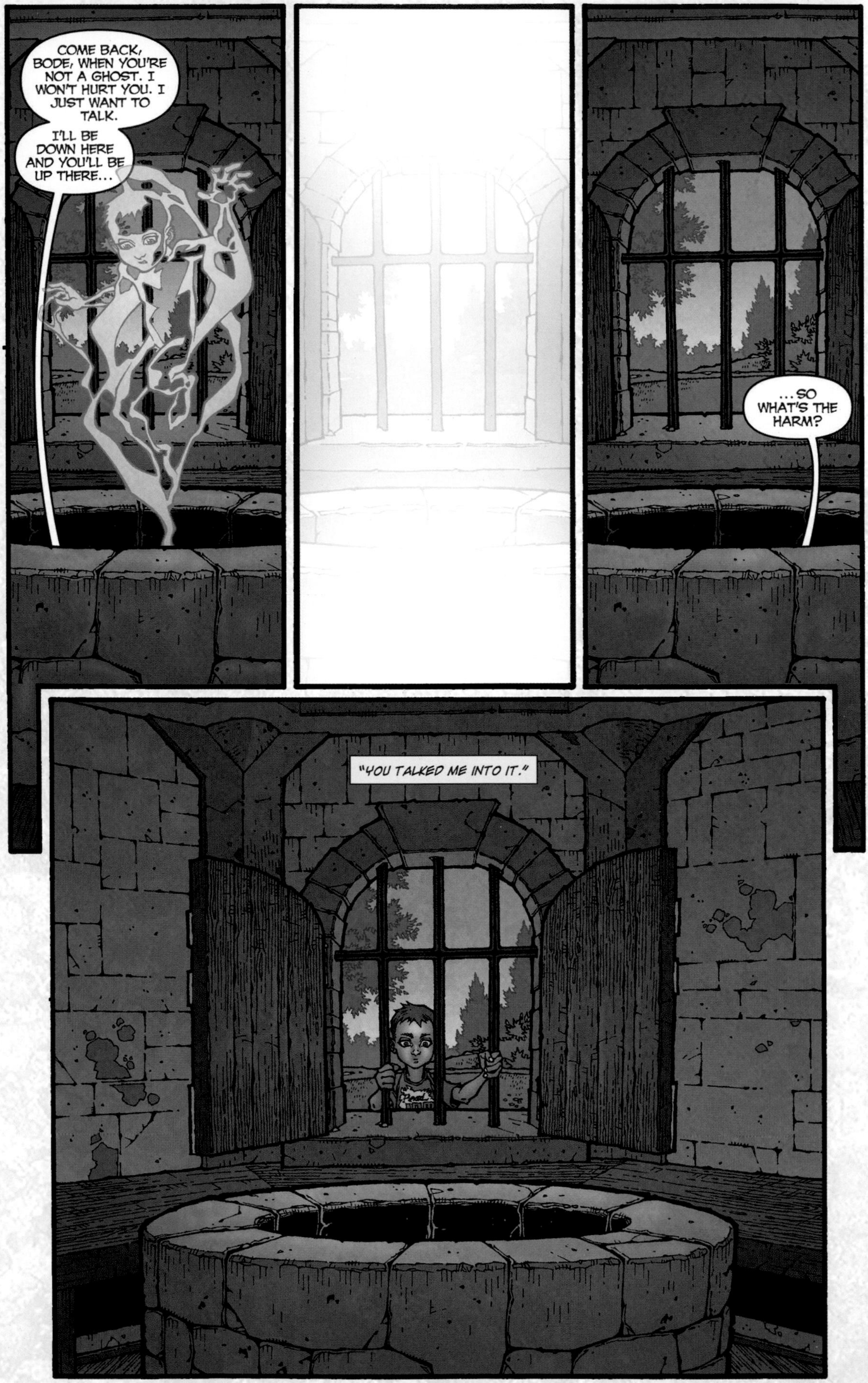
COME BACK, BODE, WHEN YOU'RE NOT A GHOST. I WON'T HURT YOU. I JUST WANT TO TALK.
I'LL BE DOWN HERE AND YOU'LL BE UP THERE...
...SO WHAT'S THE HARM?
"YOU TALKED ME INTO IT."

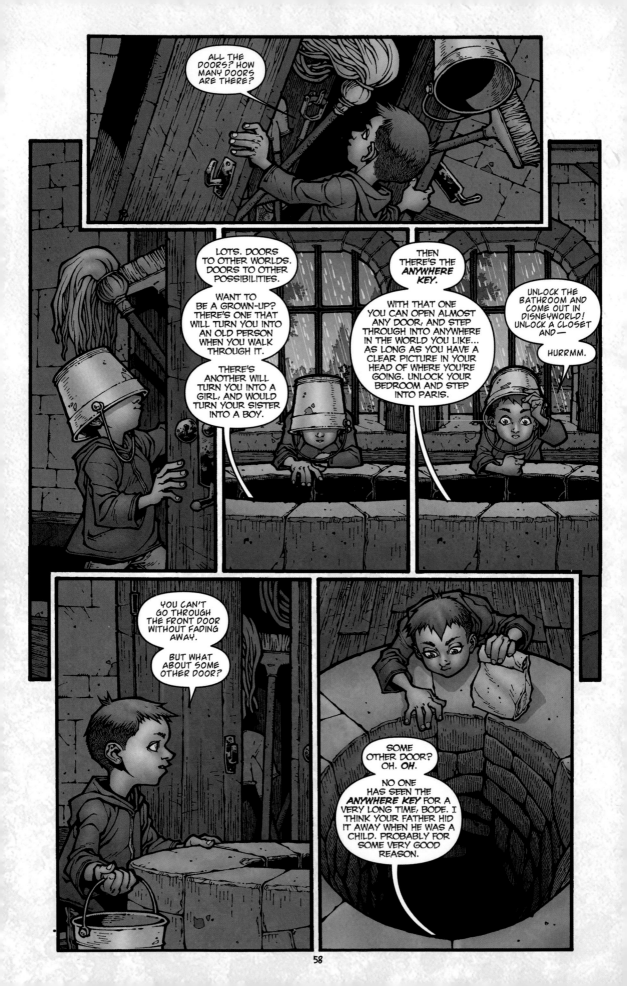

ALL THE DOORS? HOW MANY DOORS ARE THERE?

LOTS. DOORS TO OTHER WORLDS. DOORS TO OTHER POSSIBILITIES.

WANT TO BE A GROWN-UP? THERE'S ONE THAT WILL TURN YOU INTO AN OLD PERSON WHEN YOU WALK THROUGH IT.

THERE'S ANOTHER WILL TURN YOU INTO A GIRL, AND WOULD TURN YOUR SISTER INTO A BOY.

THEN THERE'S THE *ANYWHERE KEY*.

WITH THAT ONE YOU CAN OPEN ALMOST ANY DOOR, AND STEP THROUGH INTO ANYWHERE IN THE WORLD YOU LIKE... AS LONG AS YOU HAVE A CLEAR PICTURE IN YOUR HEAD OF WHERE YOU'RE GOING. UNLOCK YOUR BEDROOM AND STEP INTO PARIS.

UNLOCK THE BATHROOM AND COME OUT IN DISNEYWORLD! UNLOCK A CLOSET AND—

HURRMM.

YOU CAN'T GO THROUGH THE FRONT DOOR WITHOUT FADING AWAY.

BUT WHAT ABOUT SOME OTHER DOOR?

SOME OTHER DOOR? OH. *OH.*

NO ONE HAS SEEN THE *ANYWHERE KEY* FOR A VERY LONG TIME, BODE. I THINK YOUR FATHER HID IT AWAY WHEN HE WAS A CHILD. PROBABLY FOR SOME VERY GOOD REASON.

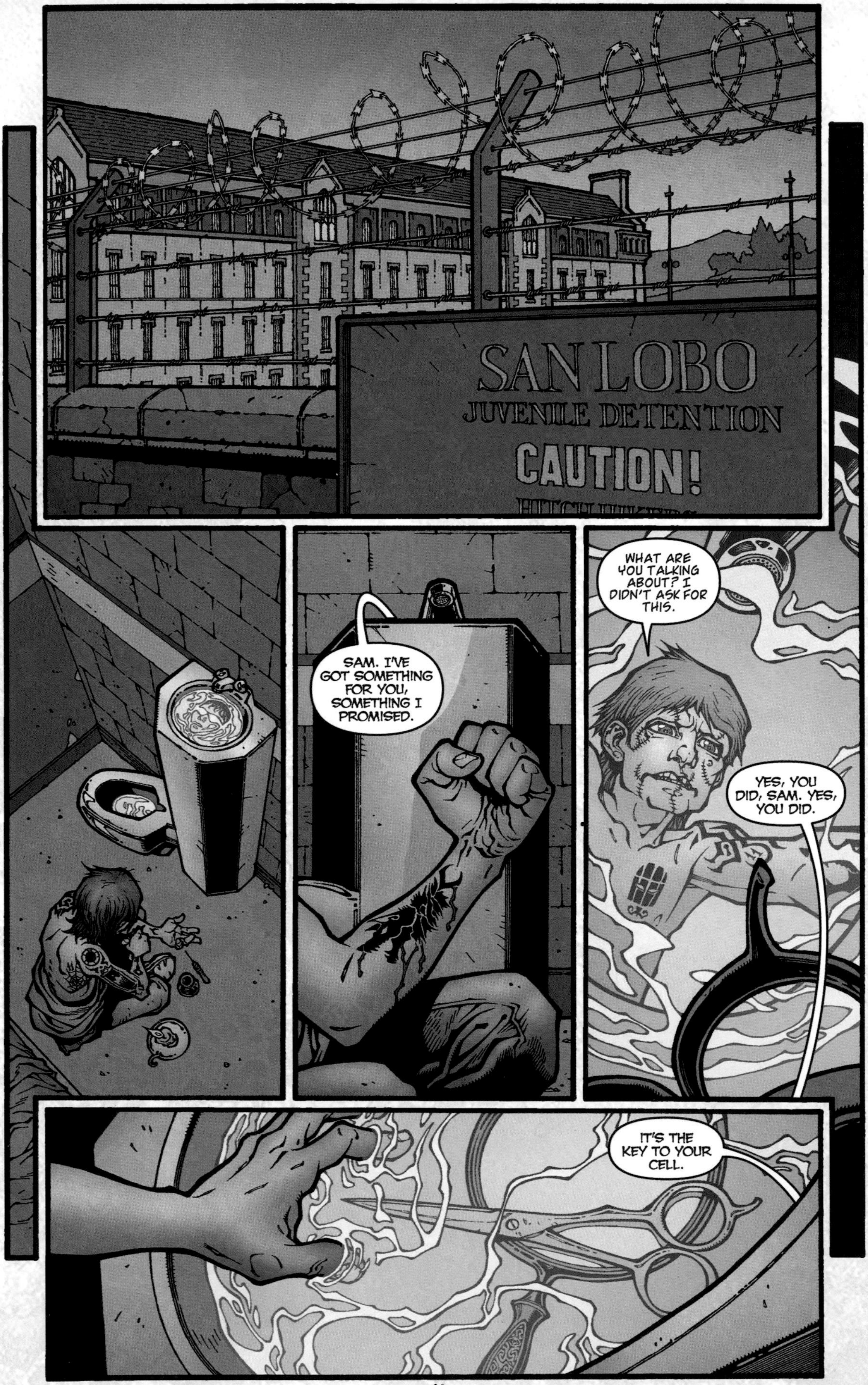
SAN LOBO
JUVENILE DETENTION
CAUTION!
SAM. I'VE GOT SOMETHING FOR YOU, SOMETHING I PROMISED.
WHAT ARE YOU TALKING ABOUT? I DIDN'T ASK FOR THIS.
YES, YOU DID, SAM. YES, YOU DID.
IT'S THE KEY TO YOUR CELL.

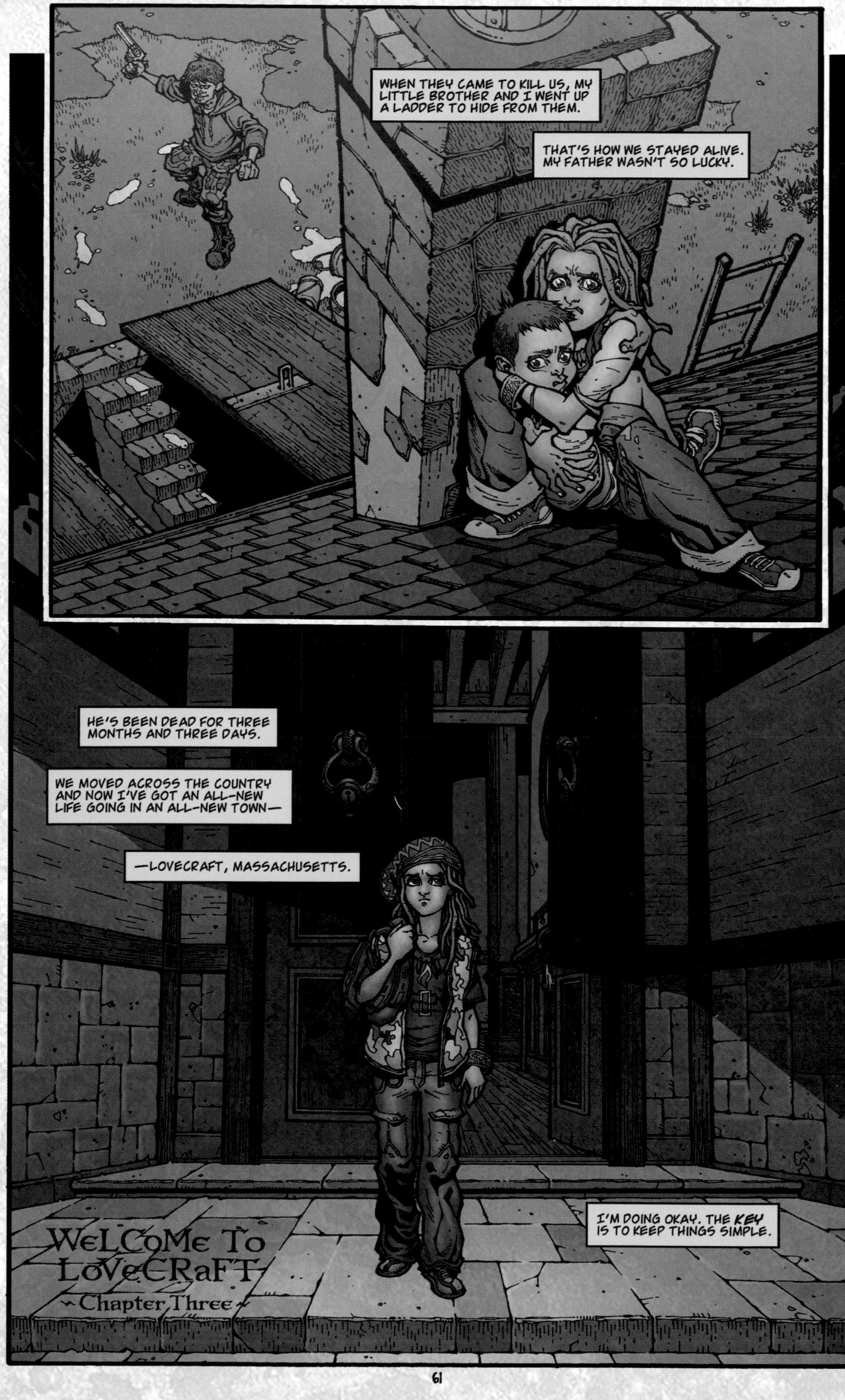
WHEN THEY CAME TO KILL US, MY LITTLE BROTHER AND I WENT UP A LADDER TO HIDE FROM THEM.
THAT'S HOW WE STAYED ALIVE. MY FATHER WASN'T SO LUCKY.
HE'S BEEN DEAD FOR THREE MONTHS AND THREE DAYS.
WE MOVED ACROSS THE COUNTRY AND NOW I'VE GOT AN ALL-NEW LIFE GOING IN AN ALL-NEW TOWN—
—LOVECRAFT, MASSACHUSETTS.
I'M DOING OKAY. THE KEY IS TO KEEP THINGS SIMPLE.
WELCOME TO LOVECRAFT
Chapter Three

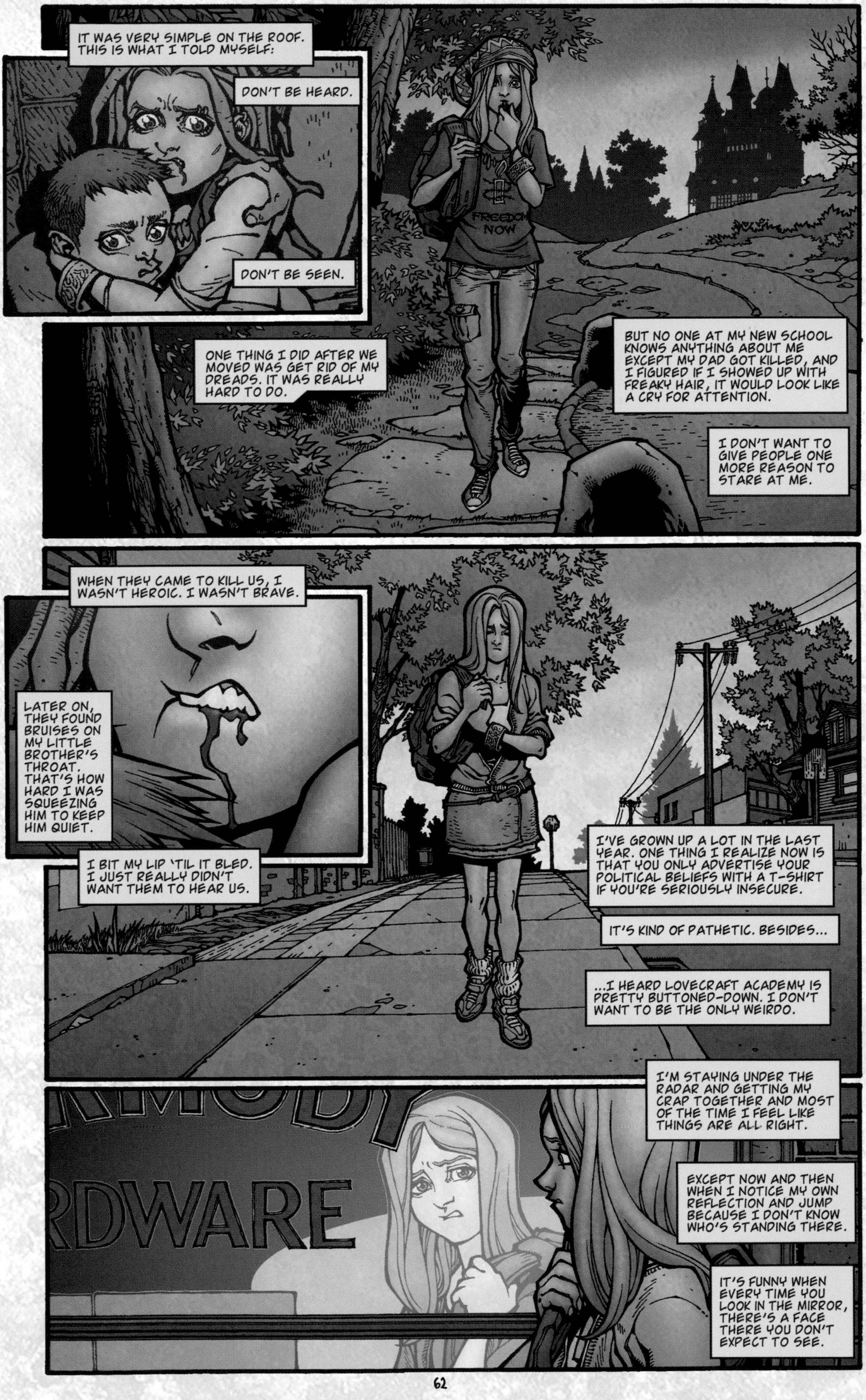
IT WAS VERY SIMPLE ON THE ROOF. THIS IS WHAT I TOLD MYSELF:
DON'T BE HEARD.
DON'T BE SEEN.
FREEDOM NOW
ONE THING I DID AFTER WE MOVED WAS GET RID OF MY DREADS. IT WAS REALLY HARD TO DO.
BUT NO ONE AT MY NEW SCHOOL KNOWS ANYTHING ABOUT ME EXCEPT MY DAD GOT KILLED, AND I FIGURED IF I SHOWED UP WITH FREAKY HAIR, IT WOULD LOOK LIKE A CRY FOR ATTENTION.
I DON'T WANT TO GIVE PEOPLE ONE MORE REASON TO STARE AT ME.
WHEN THEY CAME TO KILL US, I WASN'T HEROIC. I WASN'T BRAVE.
LATER ON, THEY FOUND BRUISES ON MY LITTLE BROTHER'S THROAT. THAT'S HOW HARD I WAS SQUEEZING HIM TO KEEP HIM QUIET.
I BIT MY LIP 'TIL IT BLED. I JUST REALLY DIDN'T WANT THEM TO HEAR US.
I'VE GROWN UP A LOT IN THE LAST YEAR. ONE THING I REALIZE NOW IS THAT YOU ONLY ADVERTISE YOUR POLITICAL BELIEFS WITH A T-SHIRT IF YOU'RE SERIOUSLY INSECURE.
IT'S KIND OF PATHETIC. BESIDES...
...I HEARD LOVECRAFT ACADEMY IS PRETTY BUTTONED-DOWN. I DON'T WANT TO BE THE ONLY WEIRDO.
I'M STAYING UNDER THE RADAR AND GETTING MY CRAP TOGETHER AND MOST OF THE TIME I FEEL LIKE THINGS ARE ALL RIGHT.
RMODY
RDWARE
EXCEPT NOW AND THEN WHEN I NOTICE MY OWN REFLECTION AND JUMP BECAUSE I DON'T KNOW WHO'S STANDING THERE.
IT'S FUNNY WHEN EVERY TIME YOU LOOK IN THE MIRROR, THERE'S A FACE THERE YOU DON'T EXPECT TO SEE.

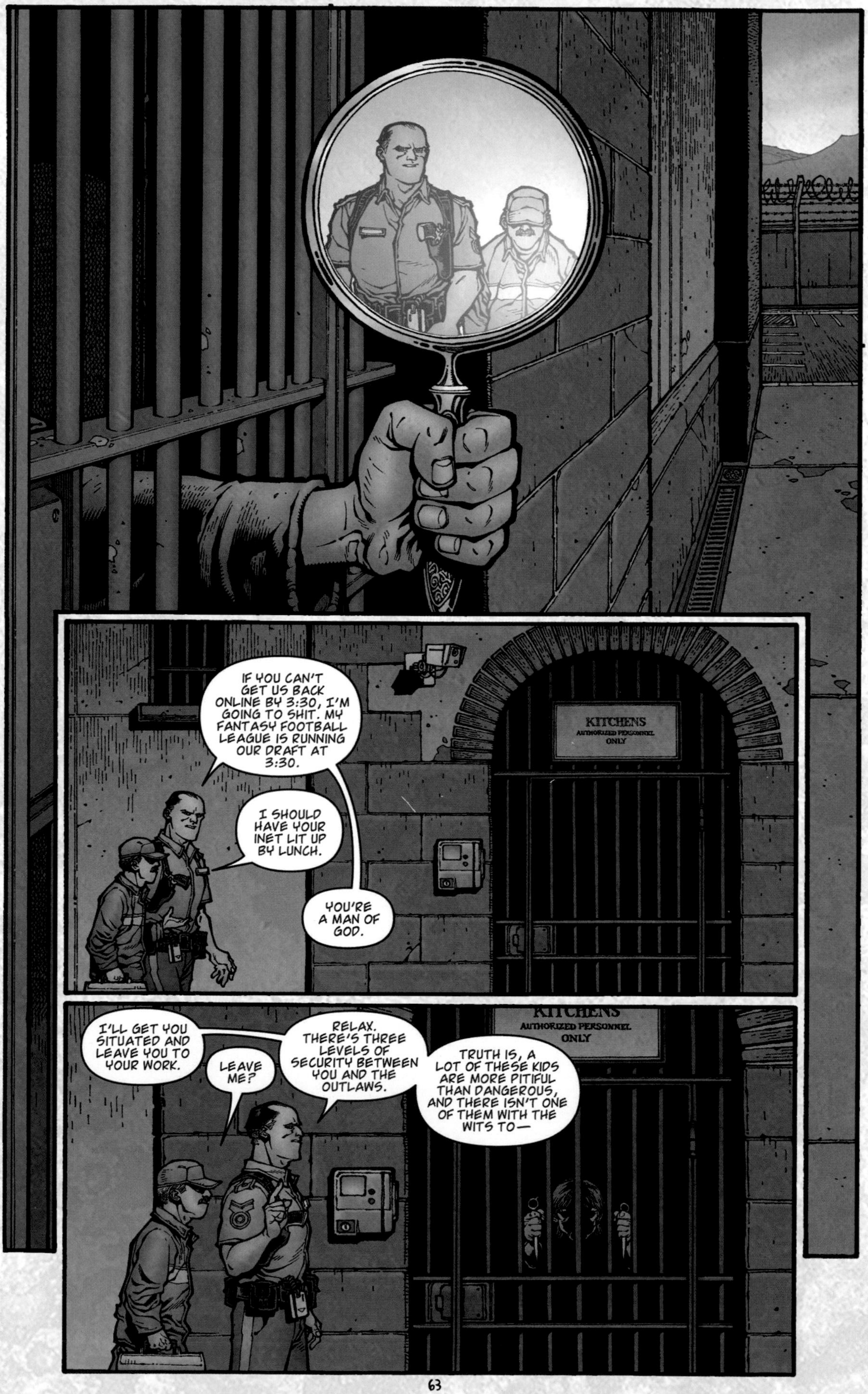
KITCHENS AUTHORIZED PERSONNEL ONLY
IF YOU CAN'T GET US BACK ONLINE BY 3:30, I'M GOING TO SHIT. MY FANTASY FOOTBALL LEAGUE IS RUNNING OUR DRAFT AT 3:30.
I SHOULD HAVE YOUR INET LIT UP BY LUNCH.
YOU'RE A MAN OF GOD.
I'LL GET YOU SITUATED AND LEAVE YOU TO YOUR WORK.
LEAVE ME?
RELAX. THERE'S THREE LEVELS OF SECURITY BETWEEN YOU AND THE OUTLAWS.
TRUTH IS, A LOT OF THESE KIDS ARE MORE PITIFUL THAN DANGEROUS, AND THERE ISN'T ONE OF THEM WITH THE WITS TO—

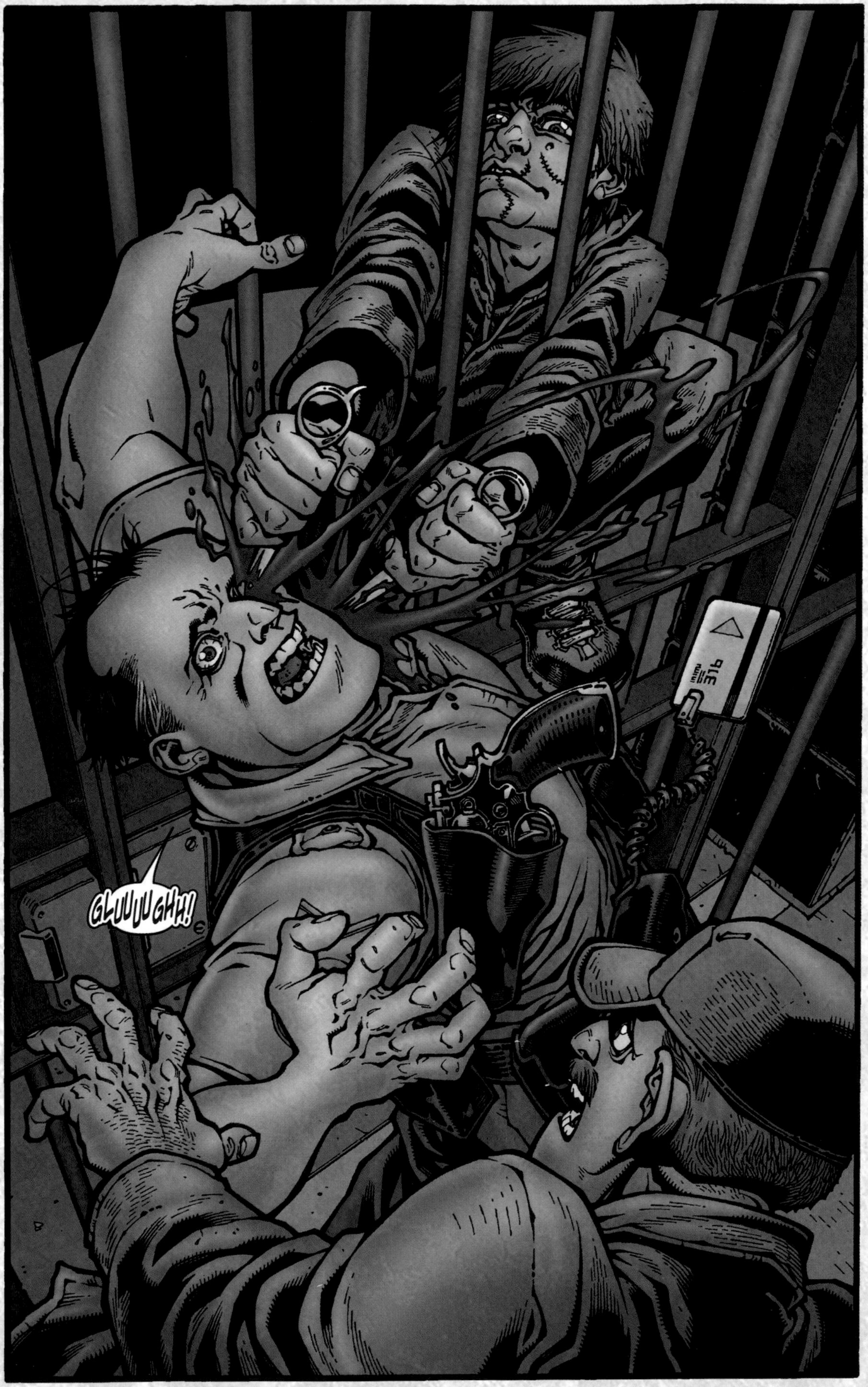
GLUUUUGHH!
316

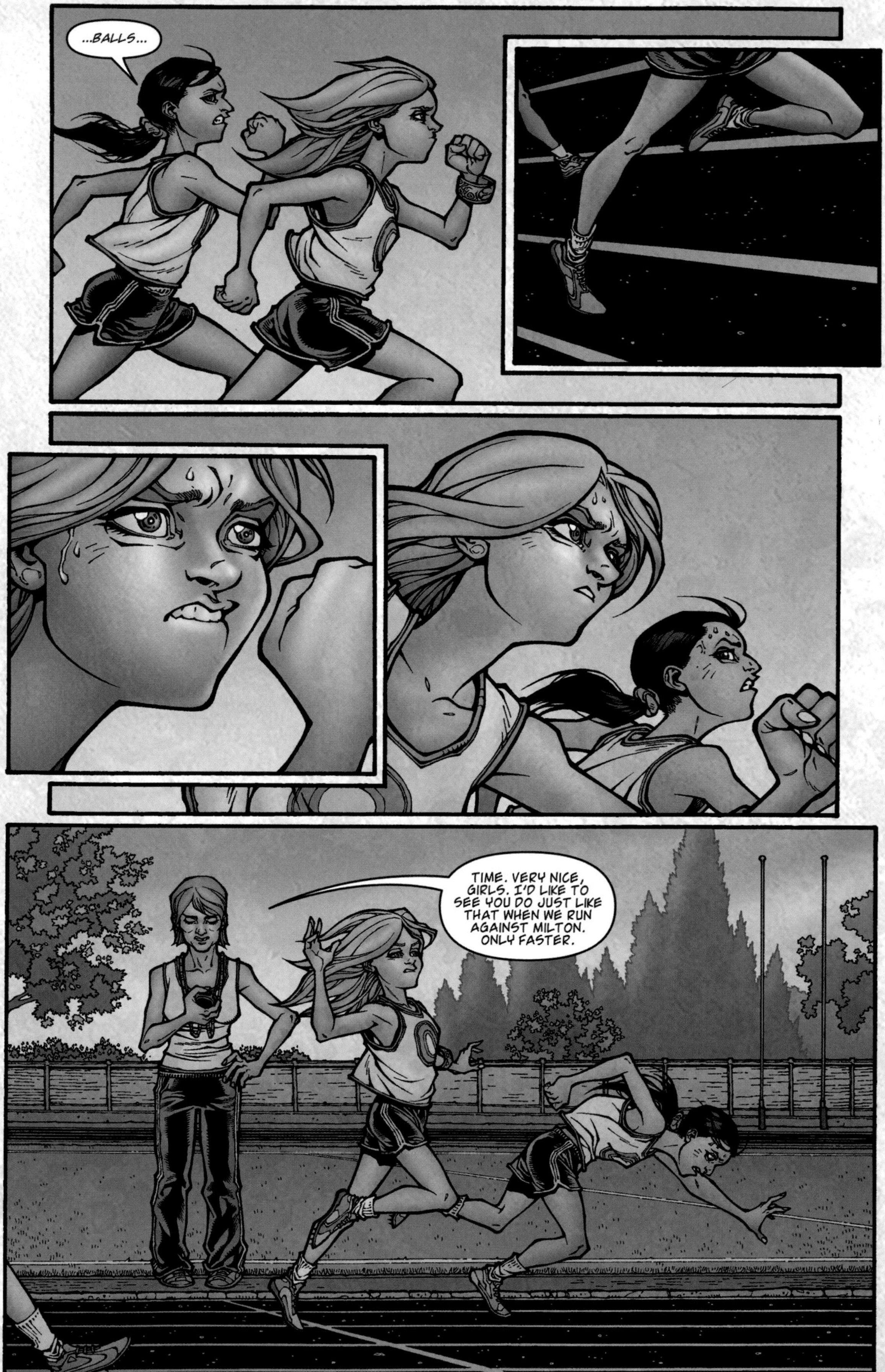
...BALLS...
TIME. VERY NICE, GIRLS. I'D LIKE TO SEE YOU DO JUST LIKE THAT WHEN WE RUN AGAINST MILTON. ONLY FASTER.

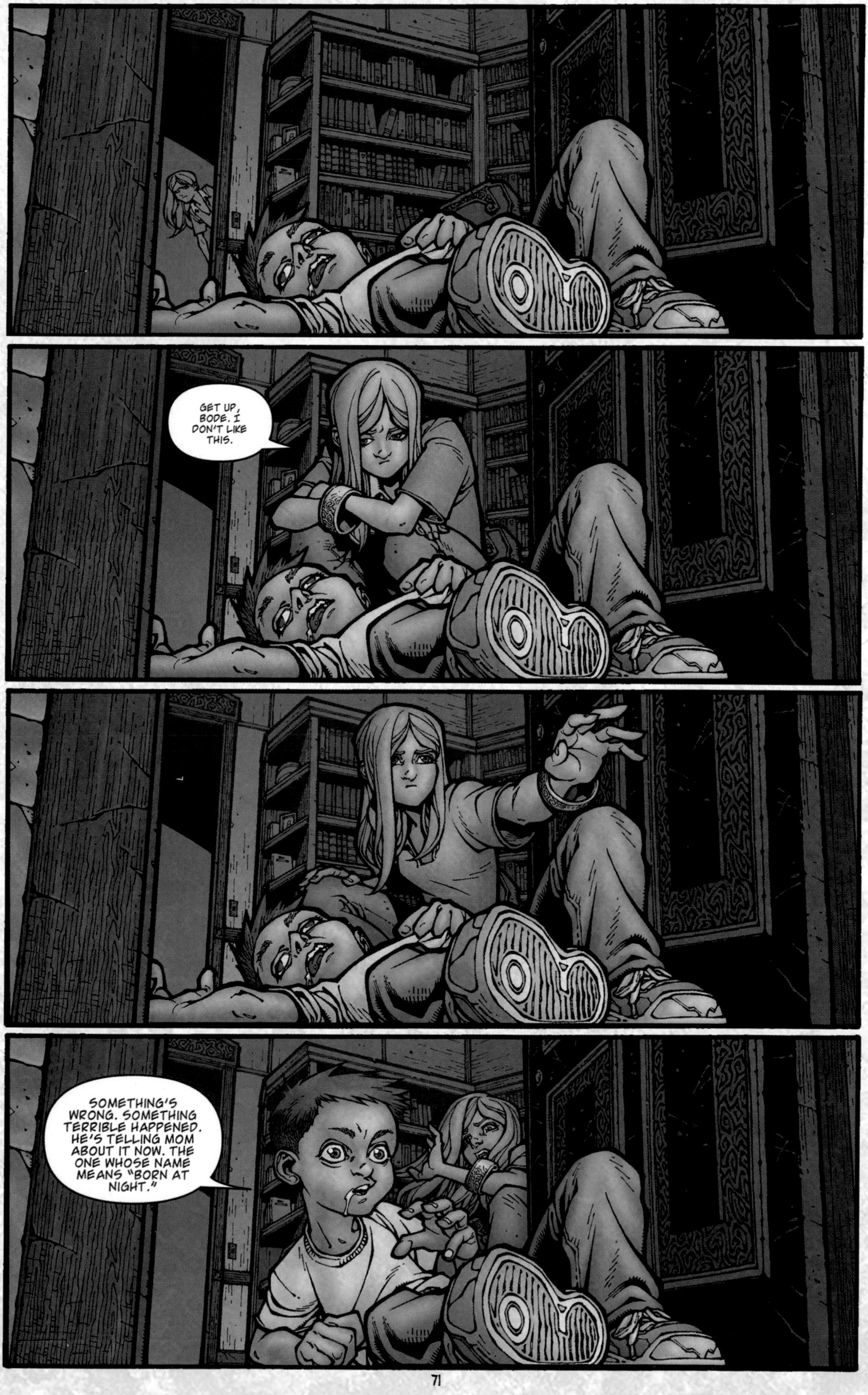
GET UP, BODE. I DON'T LIKE THIS.
SOMETHING'S WRONG. SOMETHING TERRIBLE HAPPENED. HE'S TELLING MOM ABOUT IT NOW. THE ONE WHOSE NAME MEANS "BORN AT NIGHT."

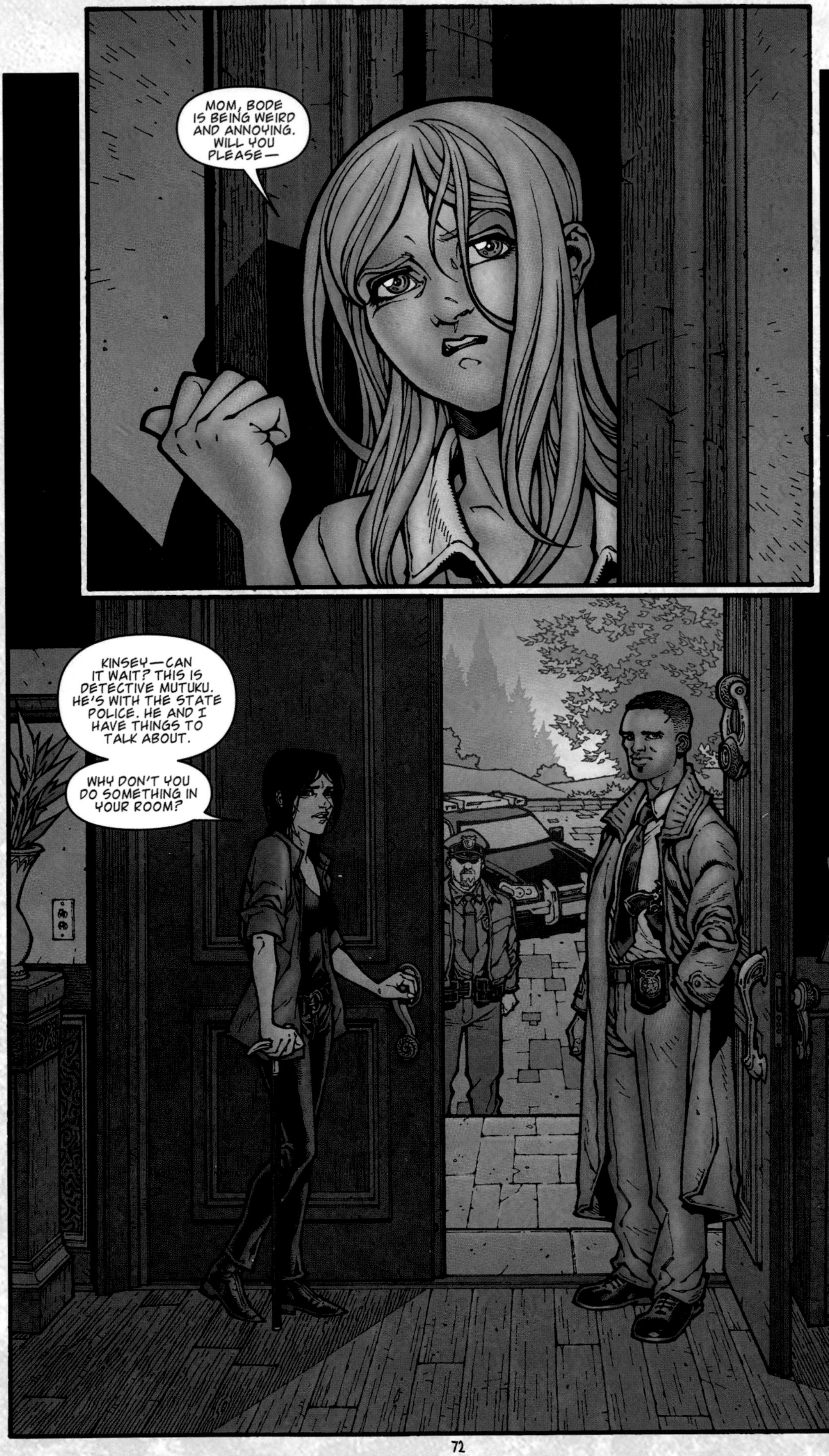
MOM, BODE IS BEING WEIRD AND ANNOYING. WILL YOU PLEASE—
KINSEY—CAN IT WAIT? THIS IS DETECTIVE MUTUKU. HE'S WITH THE STATE POLICE. HE AND I HAVE THINGS TO TALK ABOUT.
WHY DON'T YOU DO SOMETHING IN YOUR ROOM?

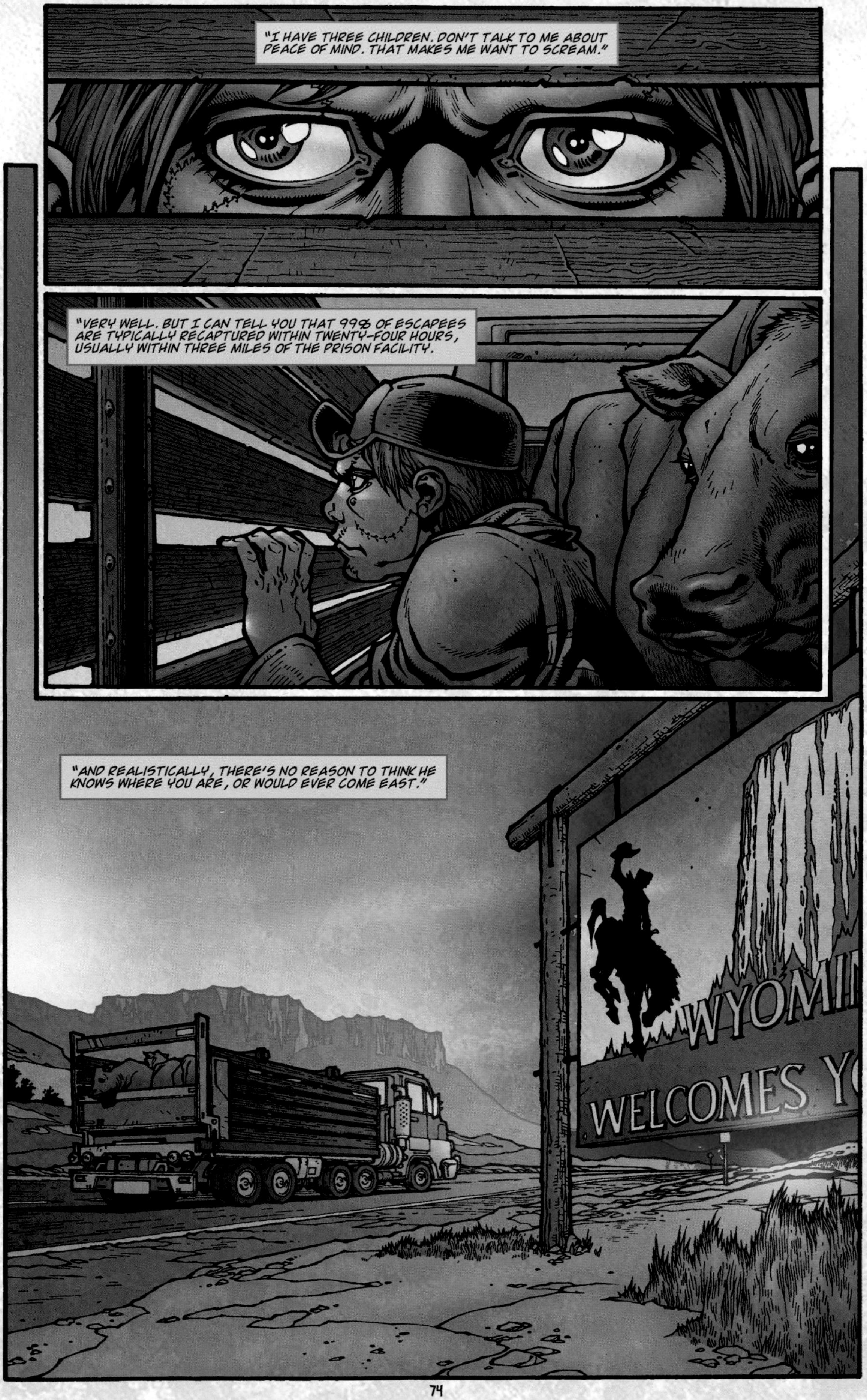
"I HAVE THREE CHILDREN. DON'T TALK TO ME ABOUT PEACE OF MIND. THAT MAKES ME WANT TO SCREAM."
"VERY WELL. BUT I CAN TELL YOU THAT 99% OF ESCAPEES ARE TYPICALLY RECAPTURED WITHIN TWENTY-FOUR HOURS, USUALLY WITHIN THREE MILES OF THE PRISON FACILITY.
"AND REALISTICALLY, THERE'S NO REASON TO THINK HE KNOWS WHERE YOU ARE, OR WOULD EVER COME EAST."

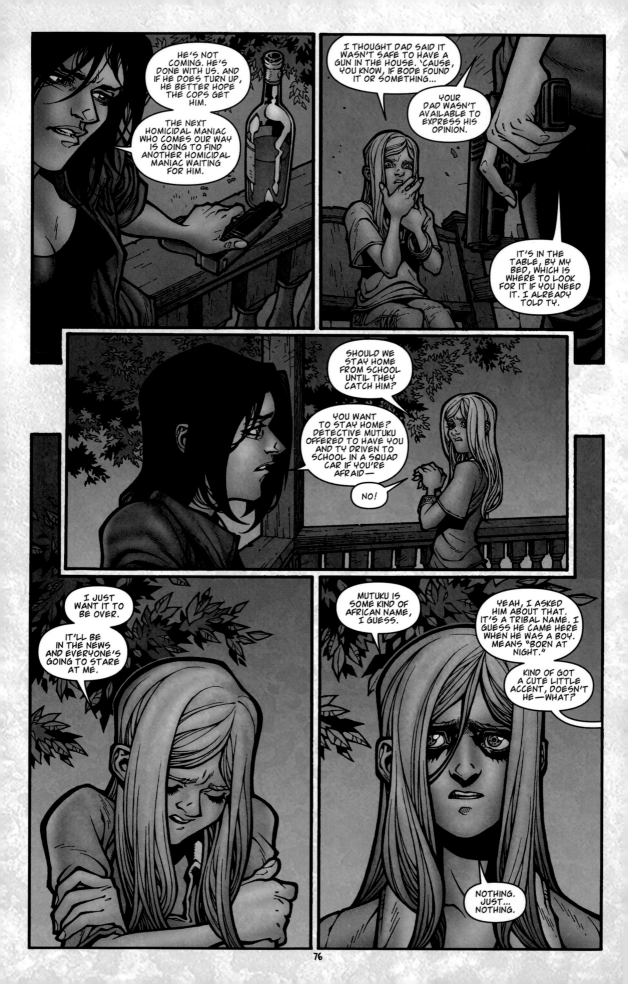

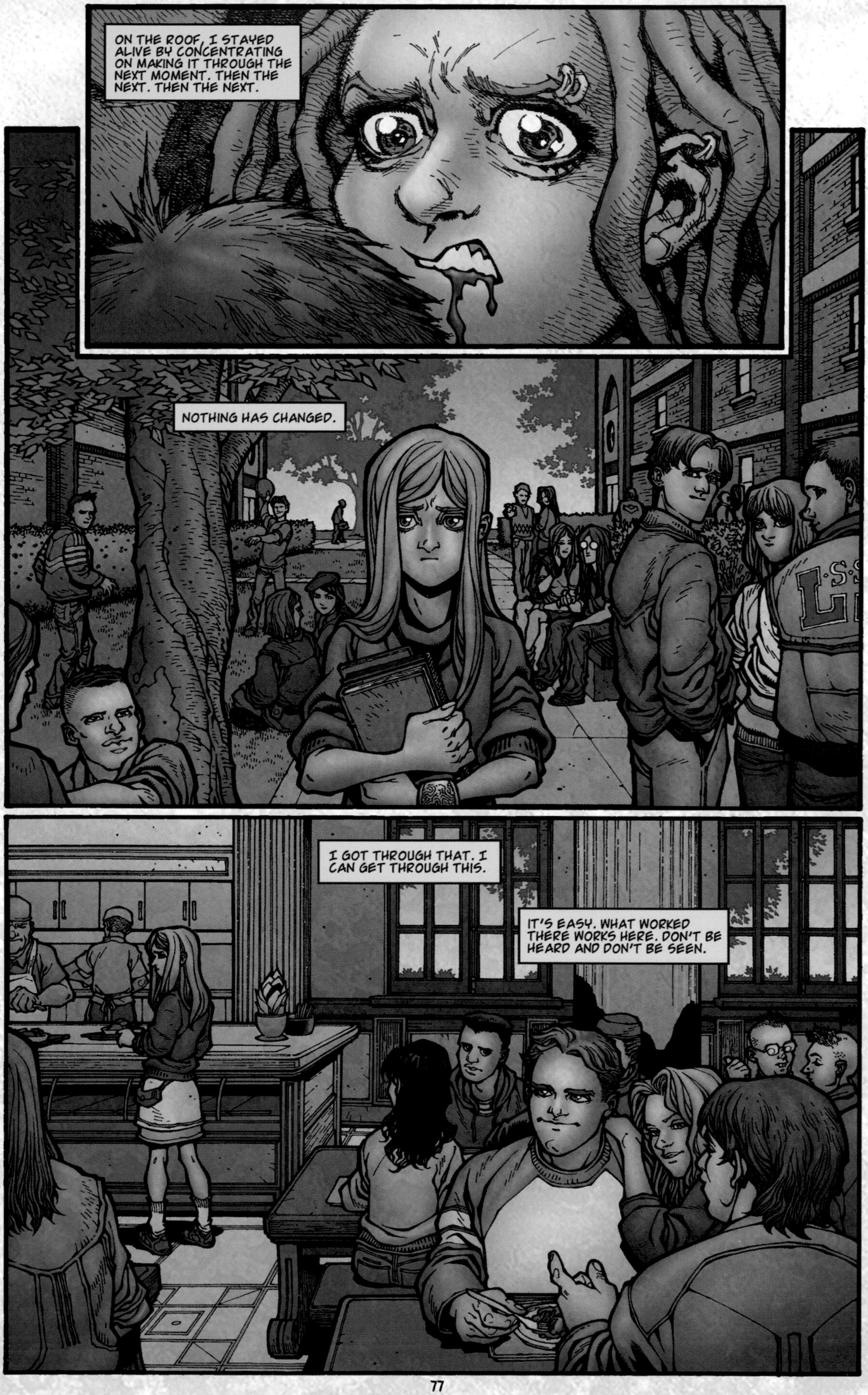

ON THE ROOF, I STAYED ALIVE BY CONCENTRATING ON MAKING IT THROUGH THE NEXT MOMENT. THEN THE NEXT. THEN THE NEXT.
NOTHING HAS CHANGED.
I GOT THROUGH THAT. I CAN GET THROUGH THIS.
IT'S EASY. WHAT WORKED THERE WORKS HERE. DON'T BE HEARD AND DON'T BE SEEN.

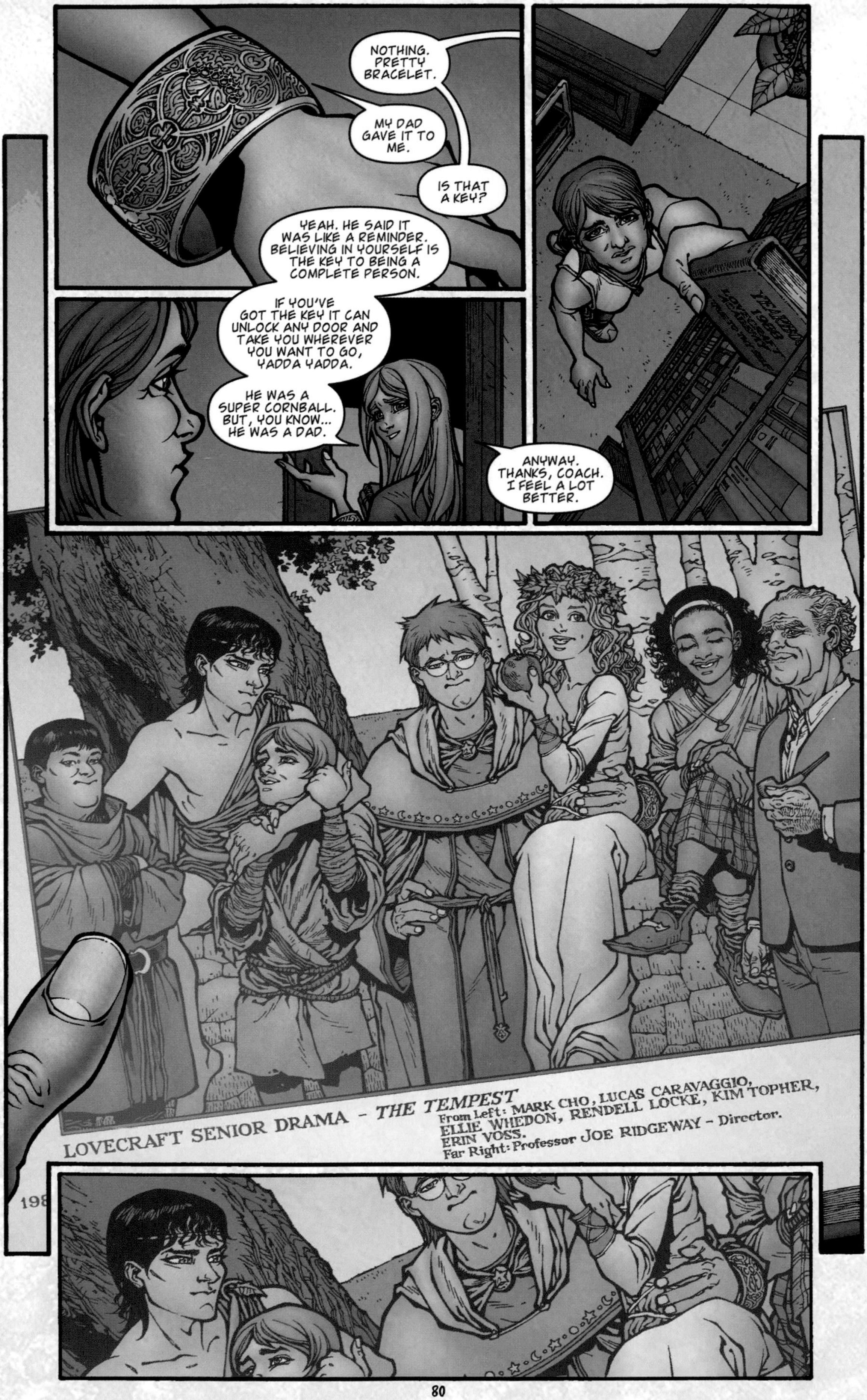

NOTHING. PRETTY BRACELET.
MY DAD GAVE IT TO ME.
IS THAT A KEY?
YEAH. HE SAID IT WAS LIKE A REMINDER. BELIEVING IN YOURSELF IS THE KEY TO BEING A COMPLETE PERSON.
IF YOU'VE GOT THE KEY IT CAN UNLOCK ANY DOOR AND TAKE YOU WHEREVER YOU WANT TO GO, YADDA YADDA.
HE WAS A SUPER CORNBALL. BUT, YOU KNOW... HE WAS A DAD.
ANYWAY. THANKS, COACH. I FEEL A LOT BETTER.
LOVECRAFT SENIOR DRAMA - THE TEMPEST
From Left: MARK CHO, LUCAS CARAVAGGIO, ELLIE WHEDON, RENDELL LOCKE, KIM TOPHER, ERIN VOSS.
Far Right: Professor JOE RIDGEWAY - Director.
198

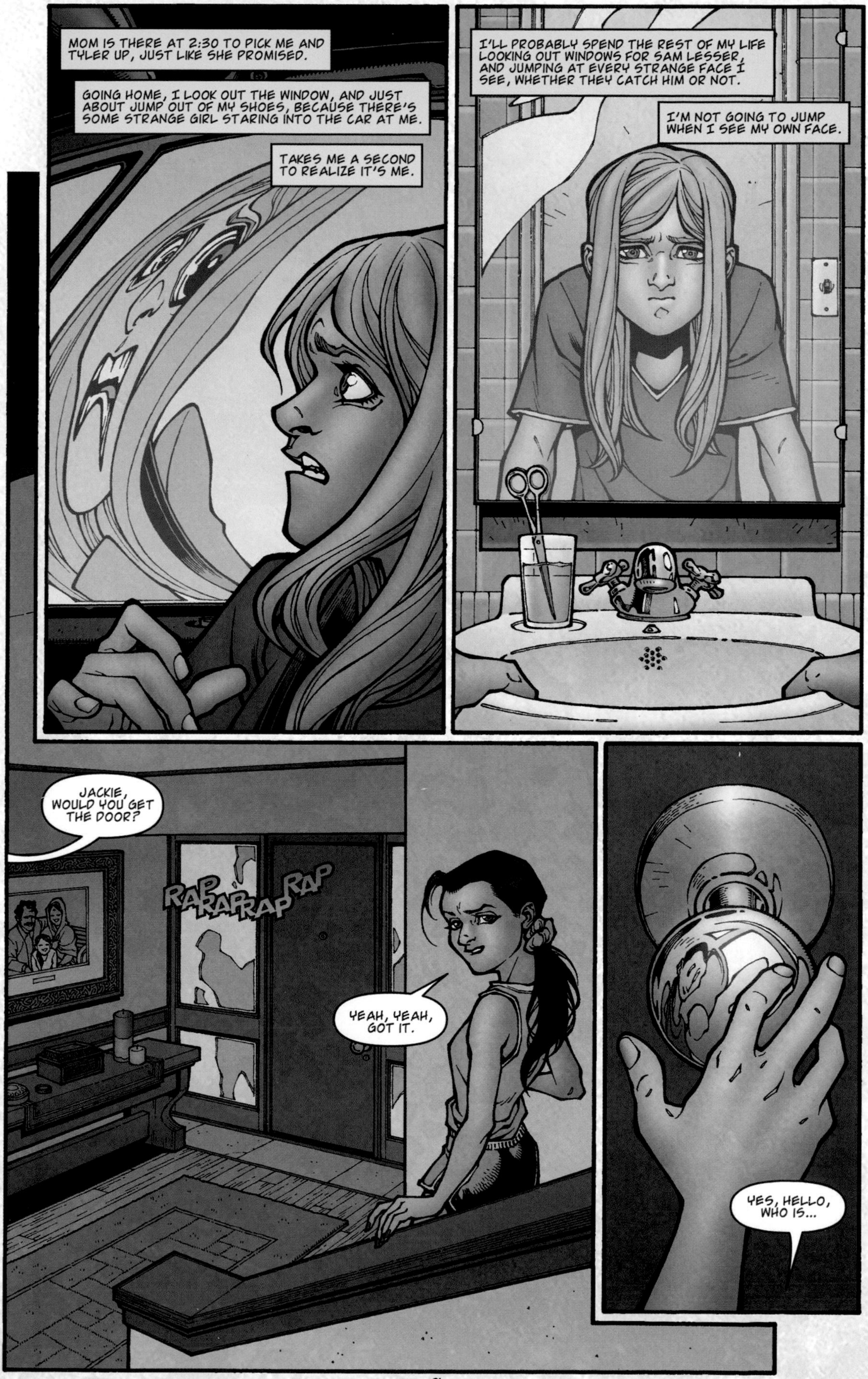

MOM IS THERE AT 2:30 TO PICK ME AND TYLER UP, JUST LIKE SHE PROMISED.
GOING HOME, I LOOK OUT THE WINDOW, AND JUST ABOUT JUMP OUT OF MY SHOES, BECAUSE THERE'S SOME STRANGE GIRL STARING INTO THE CAR AT ME.
TAKES ME A SECOND TO REALIZE IT'S ME.
I'LL PROBABLY SPEND THE REST OF MY LIFE LOOKING OUT WINDOWS FOR SAM LESSER, AND JUMPING AT EVERY STRANGE FACE I SEE, WHETHER THEY CATCH HIM OR NOT.
I'M NOT GOING TO JUMP WHEN I SEE MY OWN FACE.
JACKIE, WOULD YOU GET THE DOOR?
RAP RAP RAP RAP
YEAH, YEAH, GOT IT.
YES, HELLO, WHO IS...

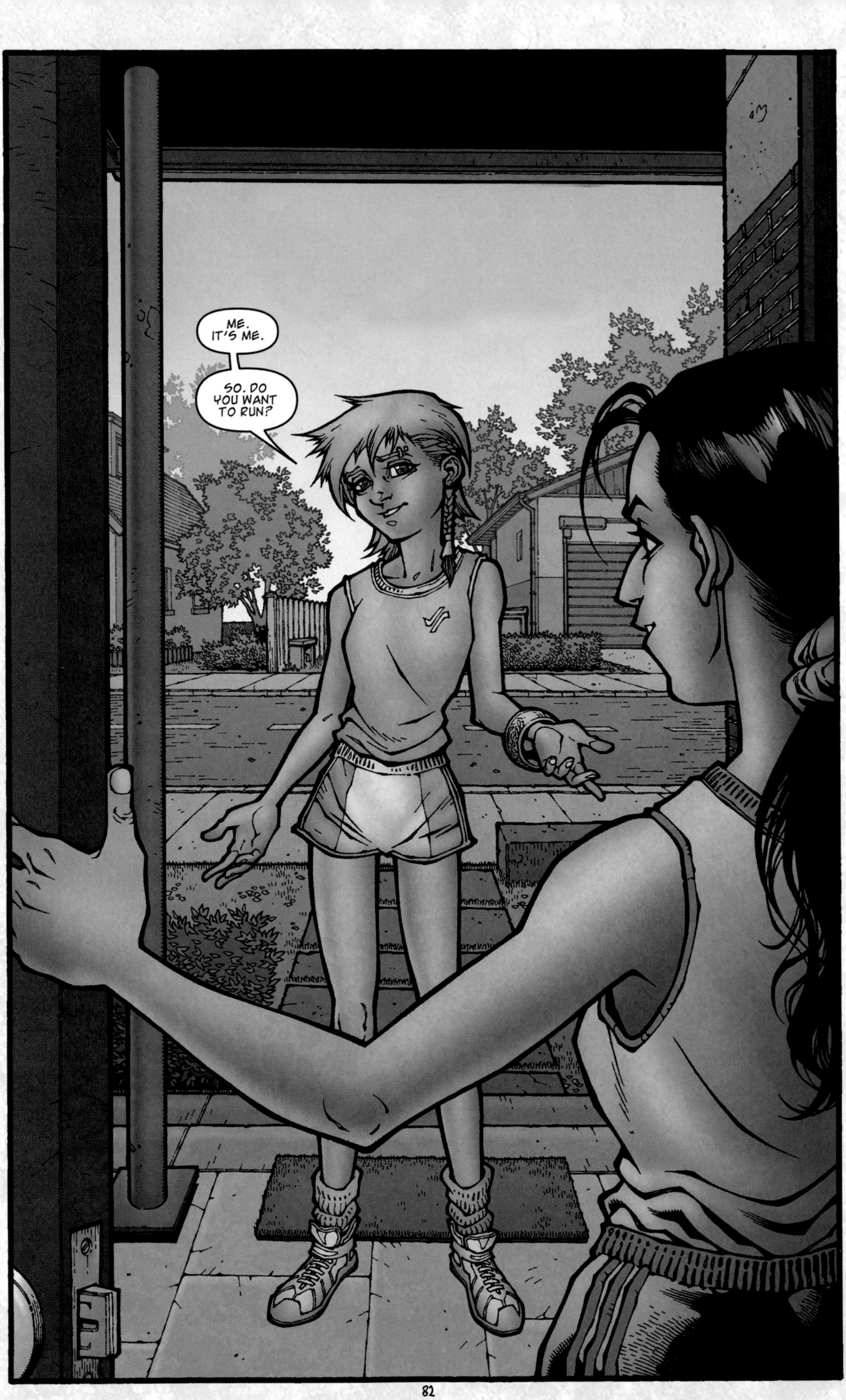
ME. IT'S ME.
SO. DO YOU WANT TO RUN?

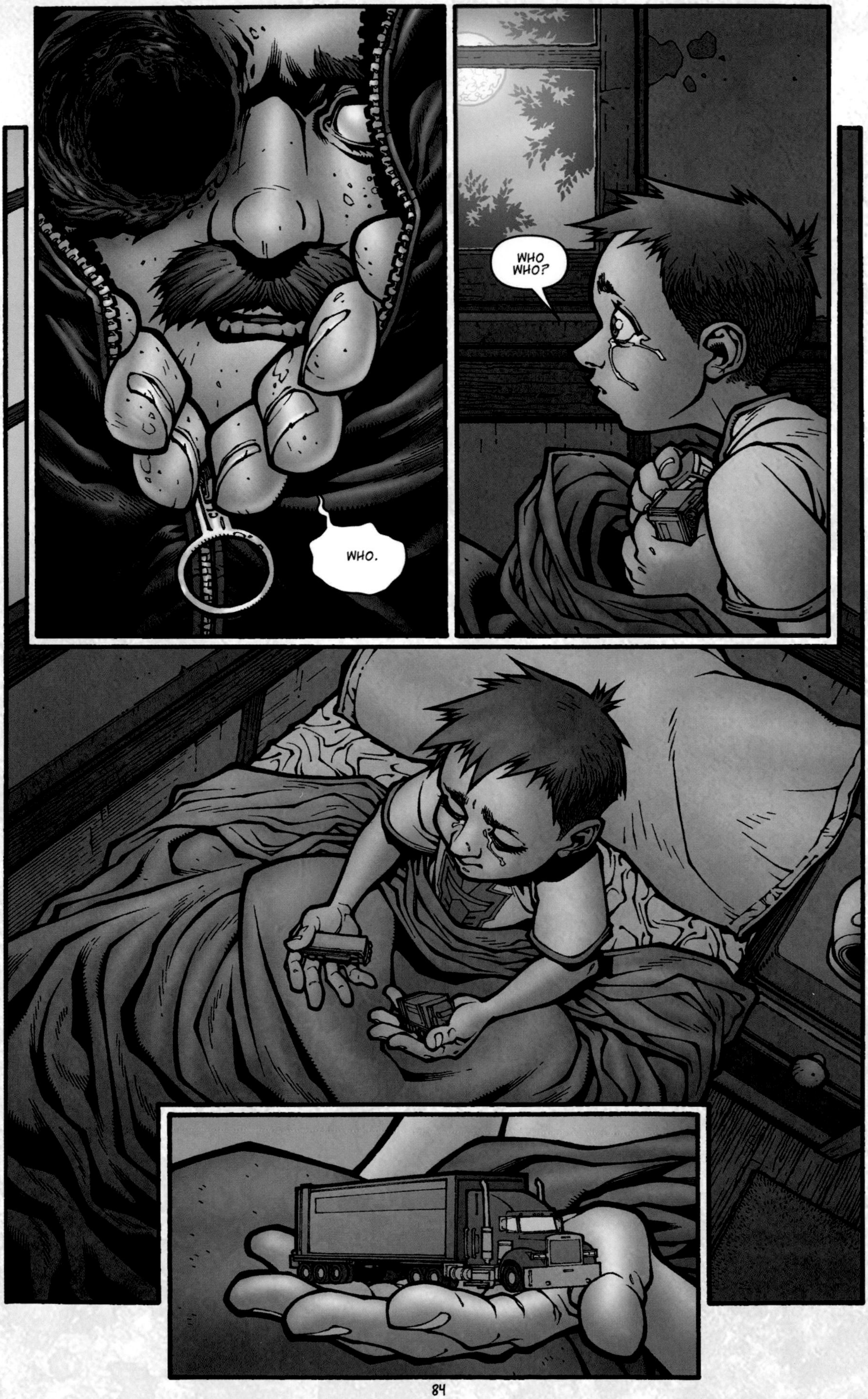
WHO WHO?
WHO.

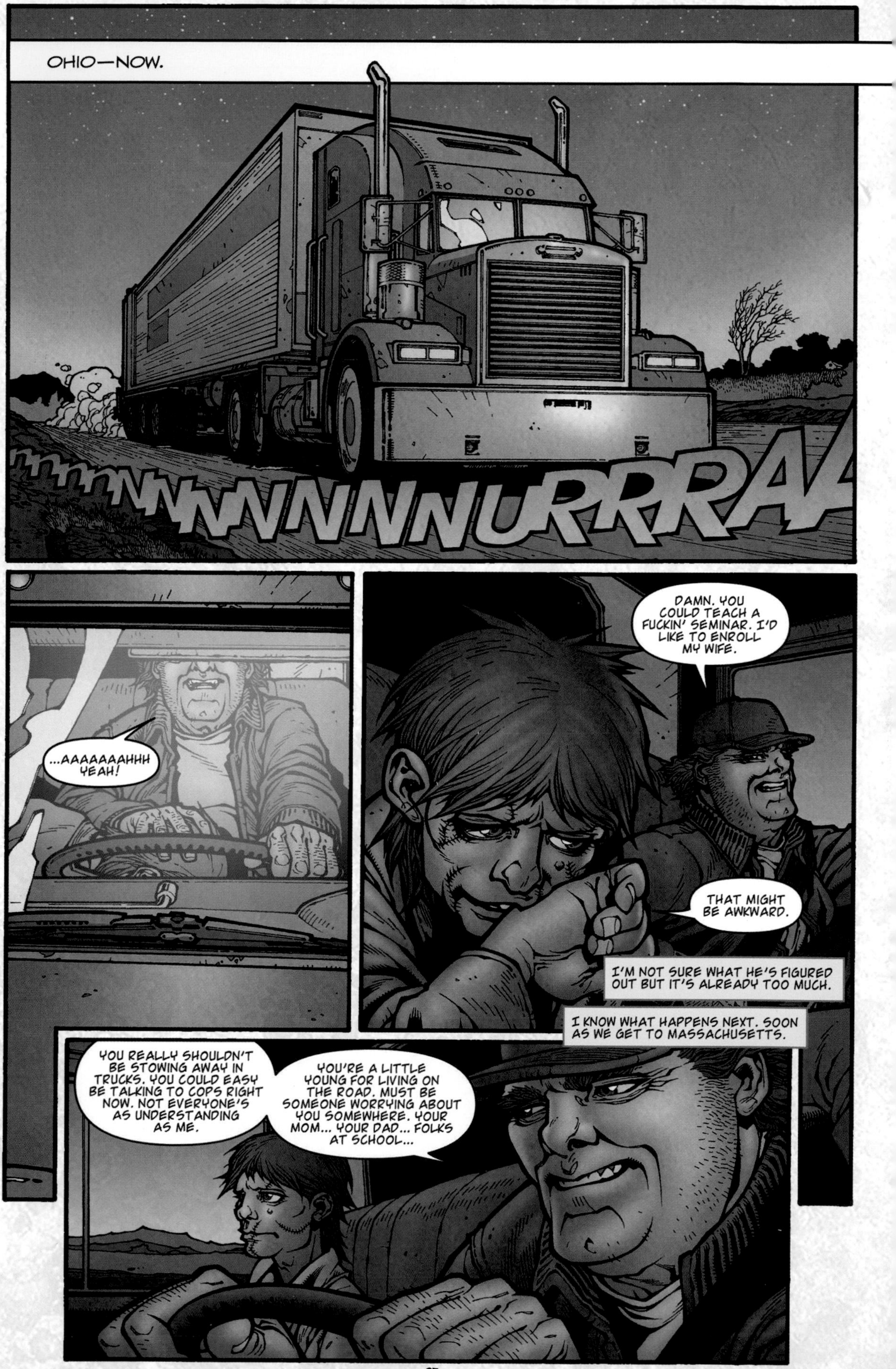
OHIO—NOW.
NNNNNNNURRRRA
...AAAAAAAHHH YEAH!
DAMN. YOU COULD TEACH A FUCKIN' SEMINAR. I'D LIKE TO ENROLL MY WIFE.
THAT MIGHT BE AWKWARD.
I'M NOT SURE WHAT HE'S FIGURED OUT BUT IT'S ALREADY TOO MUCH.
I KNOW WHAT HAPPENS NEXT. SOON AS WE GET TO MASSACHUSETTS.
YOU REALLY SHOULDN'T BE STOWING AWAY IN TRUCKS. YOU COULD EASY BE TALKING TO COPS RIGHT NOW. NOT EVERYONE'S AS UNDERSTANDING AS ME.
YOU'RE A LITTLE YOUNG FOR LIVING ON THE ROAD. MUST BE SOMEONE WORRYING ABOUT YOU SOMEWHERE. YOUR MOM... YOUR DAD... FOLKS AT SCHOOL...

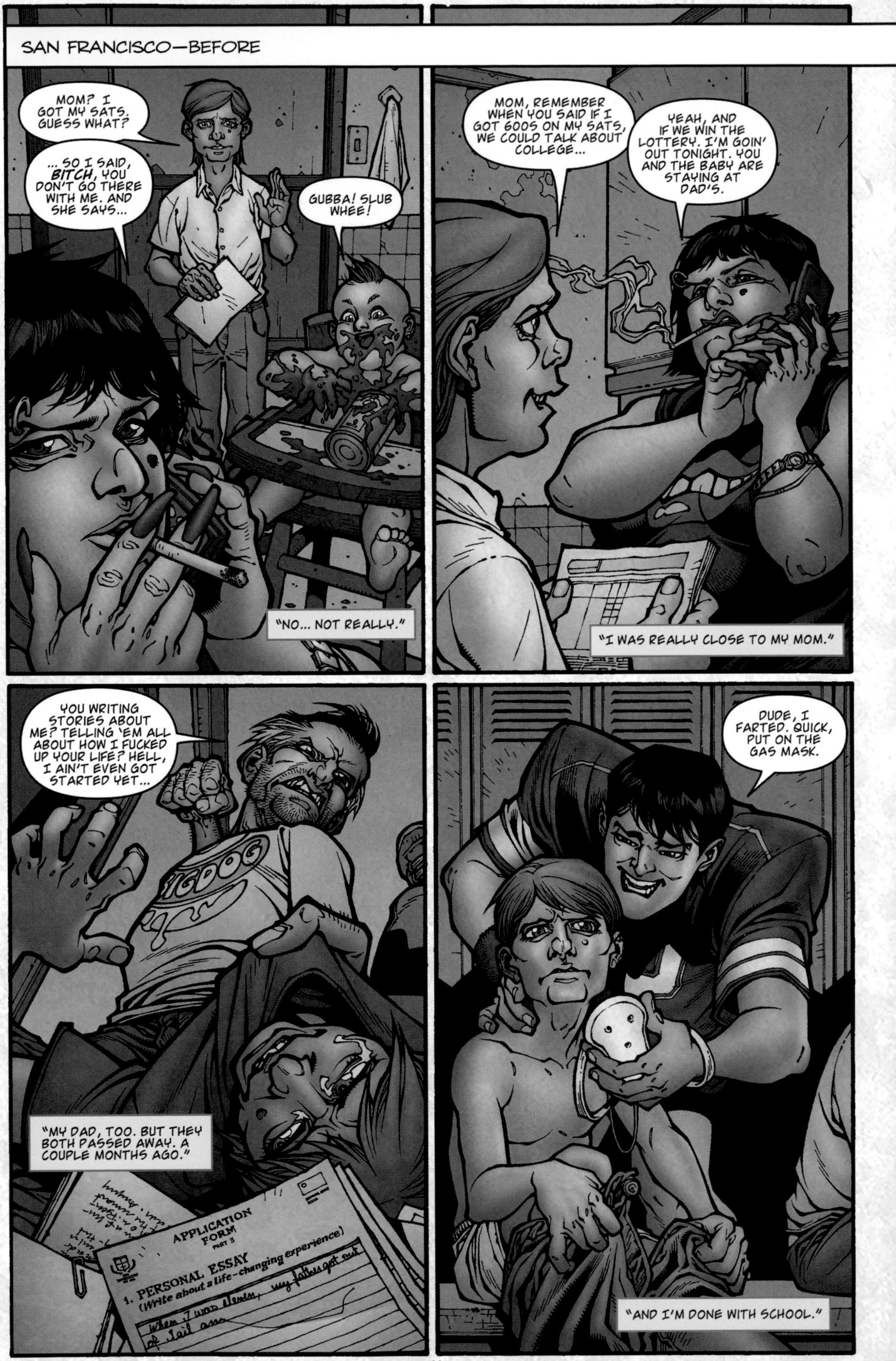
SAN FRANCISCO—BEFORE
MOM? I GOT MY SATS. GUESS WHAT?
...SO I SAID, BITCH, YOU DON'T GO THERE WITH ME. AND SHE SAYS...
GUBBA! SLUB WHEE!
"NO... NOT REALLY."
MOM, REMEMBER WHEN YOU SAID IF I GOT 600S ON MY SATS, WE COULD TALK ABOUT COLLEGE...
YEAH, AND IF WE WIN THE LOTTERY. I'M GOIN' OUT TONIGHT. YOU AND THE BABY ARE STAYING AT DAD'S.
"I WAS REALLY CLOSE TO MY MOM."
YOU WRITING STORIES ABOUT ME? TELLING 'EM ALL ABOUT HOW I FUCKED UP YOUR LIFE? HELL, I AIN'T EVEN GOT STARTED YET...
"MY DAD, TOO. BUT THEY BOTH PASSED AWAY. A COUPLE MONTHS AGO."
APPLICATION FORM
PART 3
1. PERSONAL ESSAY
(Write about a life-changing experience)
DUDE, I FARTED. QUICK, PUT ON THE GAS MASK.
"AND I'M DONE WITH SCHOOL."

EEEAAAGGGGGH!

"LOST MY TASTE FOR IT."

HEY, LESSER. I THOUGHT YOU WERE SUSPENDED FOR GOIN' RABID ON BOB MCINTYRE.

I WAS. THREE WEEKS. NOW I'M BACK.

I HEARD IT WAS LIKE *DAWN OF THE DEAD.* I HEARD IT WAS AWESOME. WHY DIN'TCHA GET EXPELLED?

RENDEL LOCKE Guidanc Counsel

MR. LOCKE BAILED ME OUT. HE SAID IT WOULD RUIN MY CHANCE AT— WHATEVER. FORGET IT.

MR. LOCKE'S PRETTY RIGHTEOUS. HE'S HELPING ME GET OUT OF THIS RETARDED SHITHOLE AND INTO VOCATIONAL.

PLUS, YOU EVER SEEN HIS WIFE?

SHE BRINGS HER CAR BY THE *RITE WASH* AND HAS ME DETAIL IT ALL THE TIME. AND SHE WEARS THESE LITTLE SKIRTS, YOU KNOW?

SHE DOES IT SO WHEN SHE GETS OUT OF HER RIDE SHE CAN OPEN HER LEGS AND FLASH ME HER PANTIES.

FIRST TIME SHE DID IT, I THOUGHT IT WAS BY ACCIDENT. AFTER FOUR OR FIVE TIMES, THOUGH, YOU KNOW WHAT SHE WANTS.

LOVECRAFT—NOW

I'VE HAD ENOUGH.

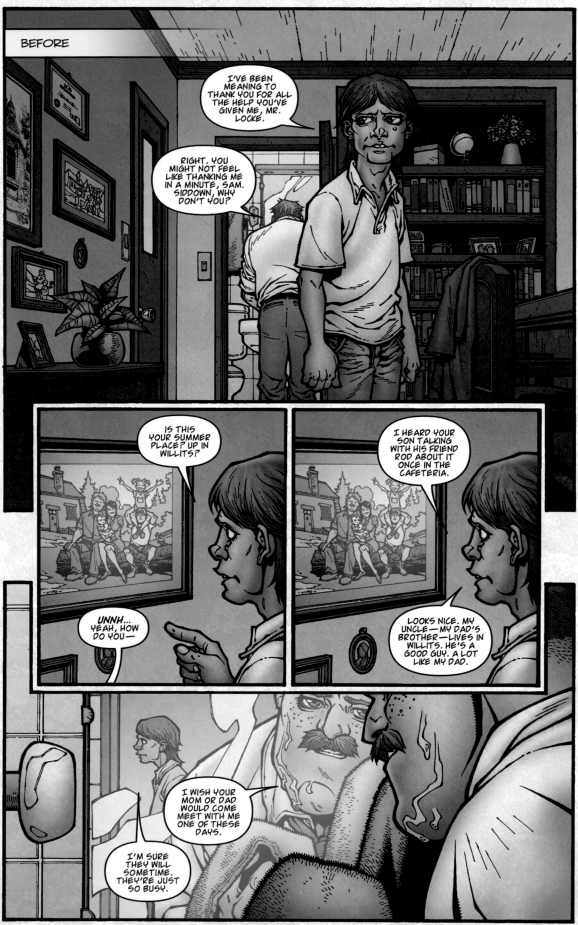

BEFORE

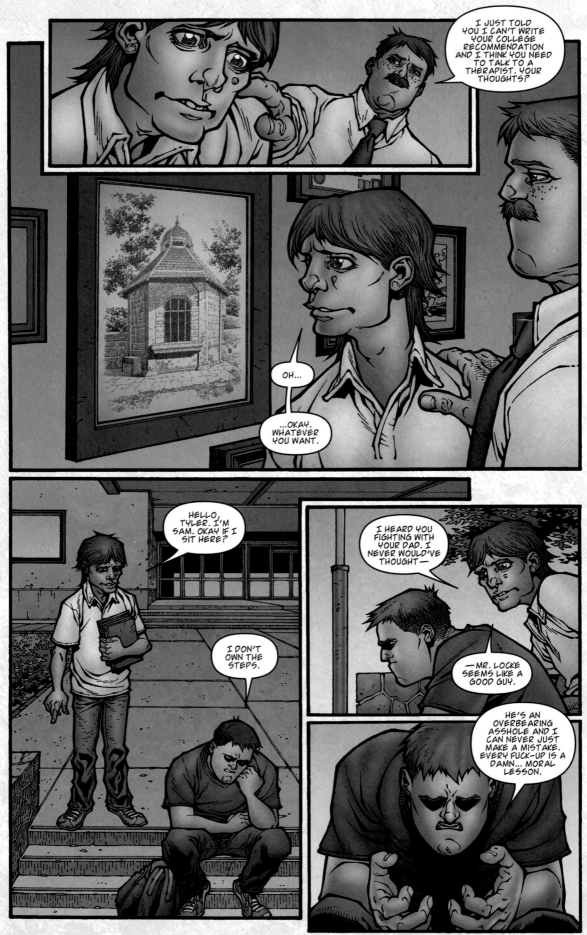

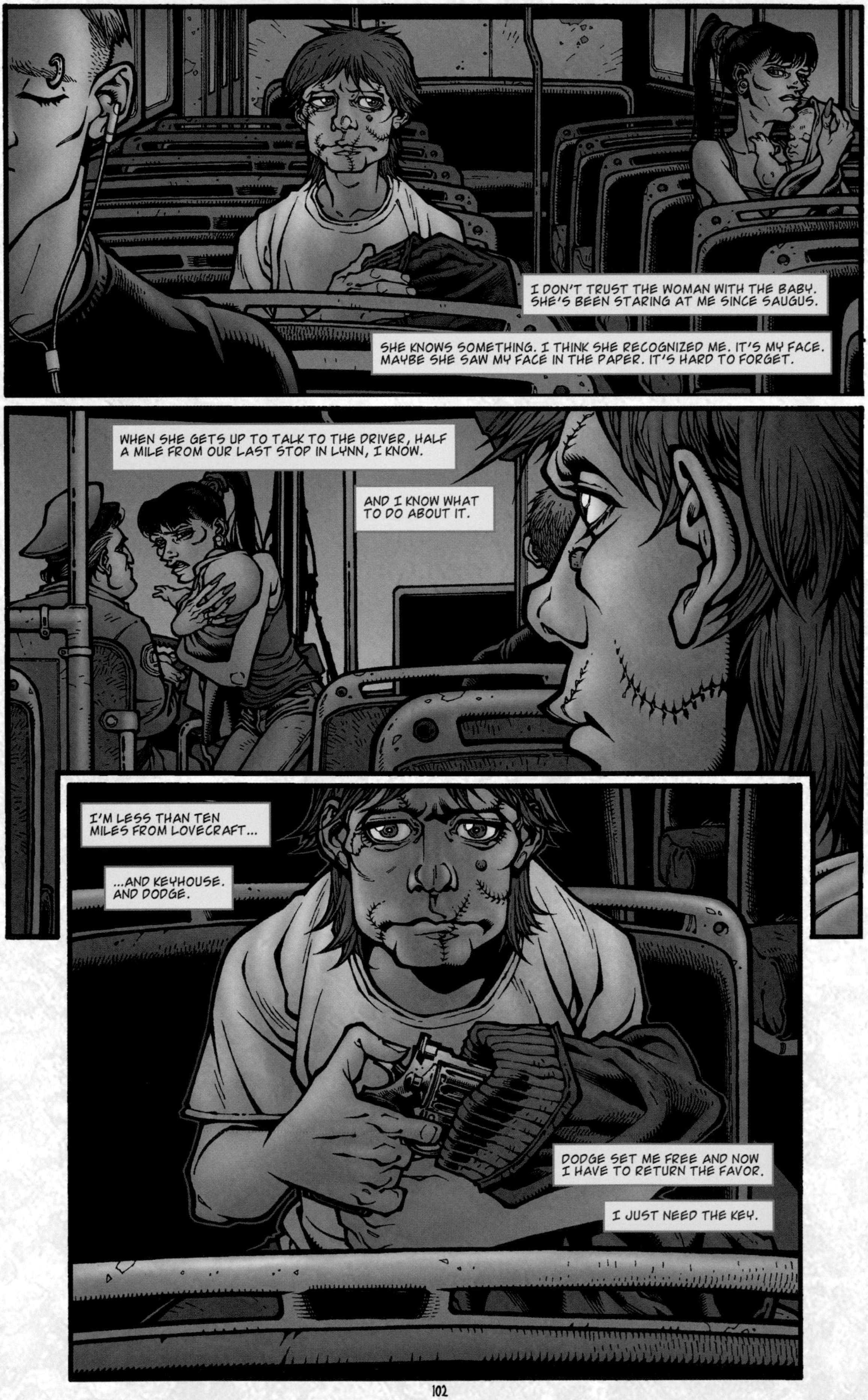
I DON'T TRUST THE WOMAN WITH THE BABY. SHE'S BEEN STARING AT ME SINCE SAUGUS.
SHE KNOWS SOMETHING. I THINK SHE RECOGNIZED ME. IT'S MY FACE. MAYBE SHE SAW MY FACE IN THE PAPER. IT'S HARD TO FORGET.
WHEN SHE GETS UP TO TALK TO THE DRIVER, HALF A MILE FROM OUR LAST STOP IN LYNN, I KNOW.
AND I KNOW WHAT TO DO ABOUT IT.
I'M LESS THAN TEN MILES FROM LOVECRAFT...
...AND KEYHOUSE. AND DODGE.
DODGE SET ME FREE AND NOW I HAVE TO RETURN THE FAVOR.
I JUST NEED THE KEY.

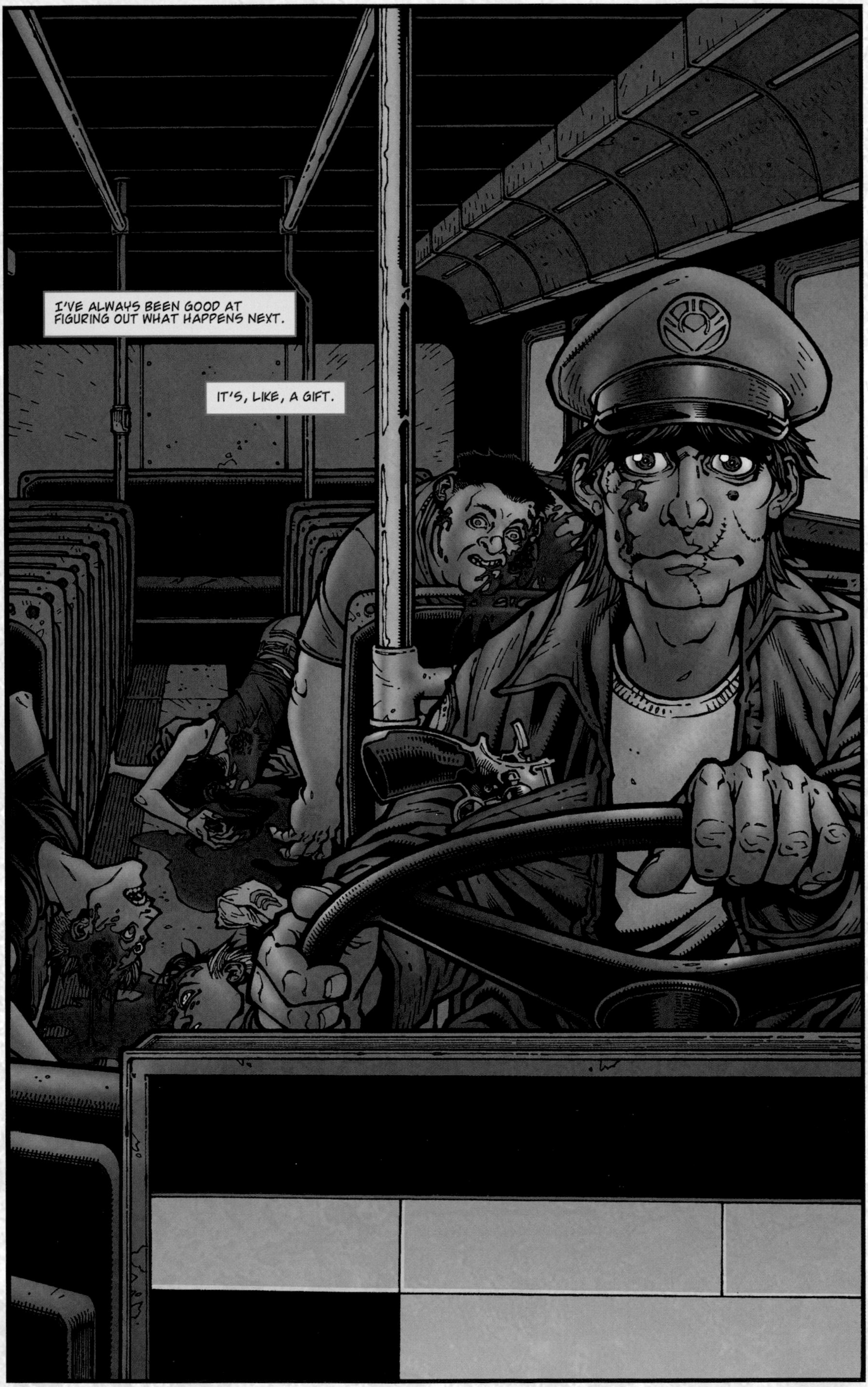
I'VE ALWAYS BEEN GOOD AT FIGURING OUT WHAT HAPPENS NEXT.
IT'S, LIKE, A GIFT.

WELCOME TO
LOVECRAFT
~Chapter Five~

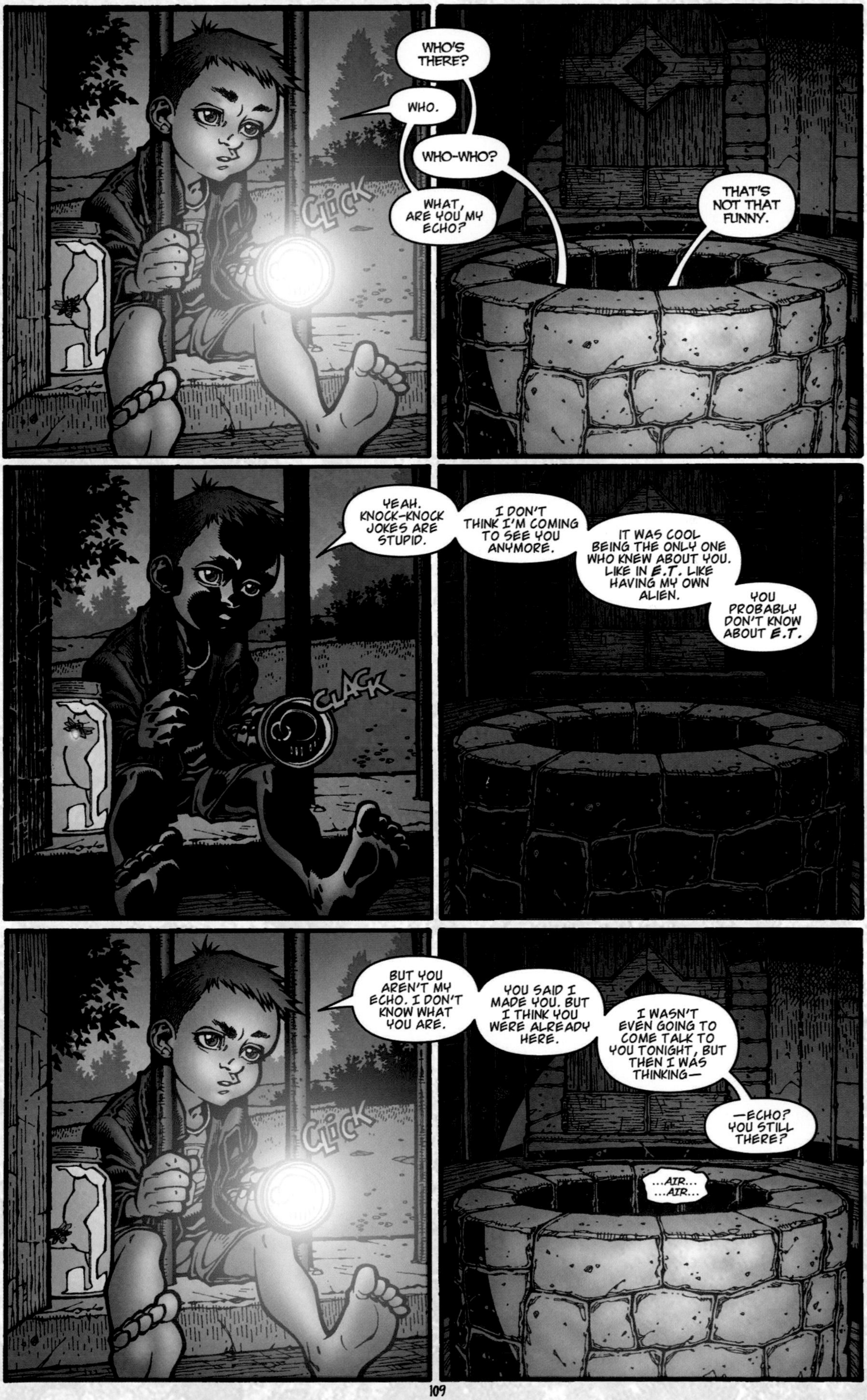
WHO'S THERE?
WHO.
WHO-WHO?
WHAT, ARE YOU MY ECHO?
THAT'S NOT THAT FUNNY.
CLICK
YEAH. KNOCK-KNOCK JOKES ARE STUPID.
I DON'T THINK I'M COMING TO SEE YOU ANYMORE.
IT WAS COOL BEING THE ONLY ONE WHO KNEW ABOUT YOU. LIKE IN E.T. LIKE HAVING MY OWN ALIEN.
YOU PROBABLY DON'T KNOW ABOUT E.T.
CLACK
BUT YOU AREN'T MY ECHO. I DON'T KNOW WHAT YOU ARE.
YOU SAID I MADE YOU. BUT I THINK YOU WERE ALREADY HERE.
I WASN'T EVEN GOING TO COME TALK TO YOU TONIGHT, BUT THEN I WAS THINKING—
—ECHO? YOU STILL THERE?
CLICK
...AIR... ...AIR...

...TEEN SUICIDE IS ON THE RISE IN THE U.S. FOR THE THIRD STRAIGHT YEAR...

T'HICK T'HICK T'HICK

ch 9

... VANDALIZED THIS SYNAGOGUE. THE BOYS RESPONSIBLE TOLD POLICE THEY DID IT ON A DARE...

...POLICE SAY HIS YOUNGEST VICTIM WAS A 13-YEAR-OLD GIRL HE MET IN AN ONLINE CHAT...

ch 9

WAR ON TERROR

...PFC LON COONEY ENLISTED AFTER HIGH SCHOOL AND WAS ONLY NINETEEN WHEN A ROADSIDE BOMB...

...MAYBE I JUST HAD THE WRONG KEY, BUT I SWEAR THE LOCKS IN THIS HOUSE HAVE MINDS OF THEIR OWN...

NO JOKE.

...DATE RAPE DRUG...

ch 9

...BEATEN INTO A COMA DURING A HAZING RITUAL...

LIVE REPORT

WHAT YOU UP TO, KID?

WATCHING THE NEWS. WAITING FOR SPORTS.

LEARN ANYTHING NEW?

NOTHING I DIDN'T ALREADY KNOW.

ch 9

...A PASSENGER BUS HAS BEEN CONSUMED BY FIRE, JUST TWO BLOCKS FROM THE BURRILL STREET STATION. NO WORD YET ON THE CAUSE BUT WE'RE GOING LIVE...

112

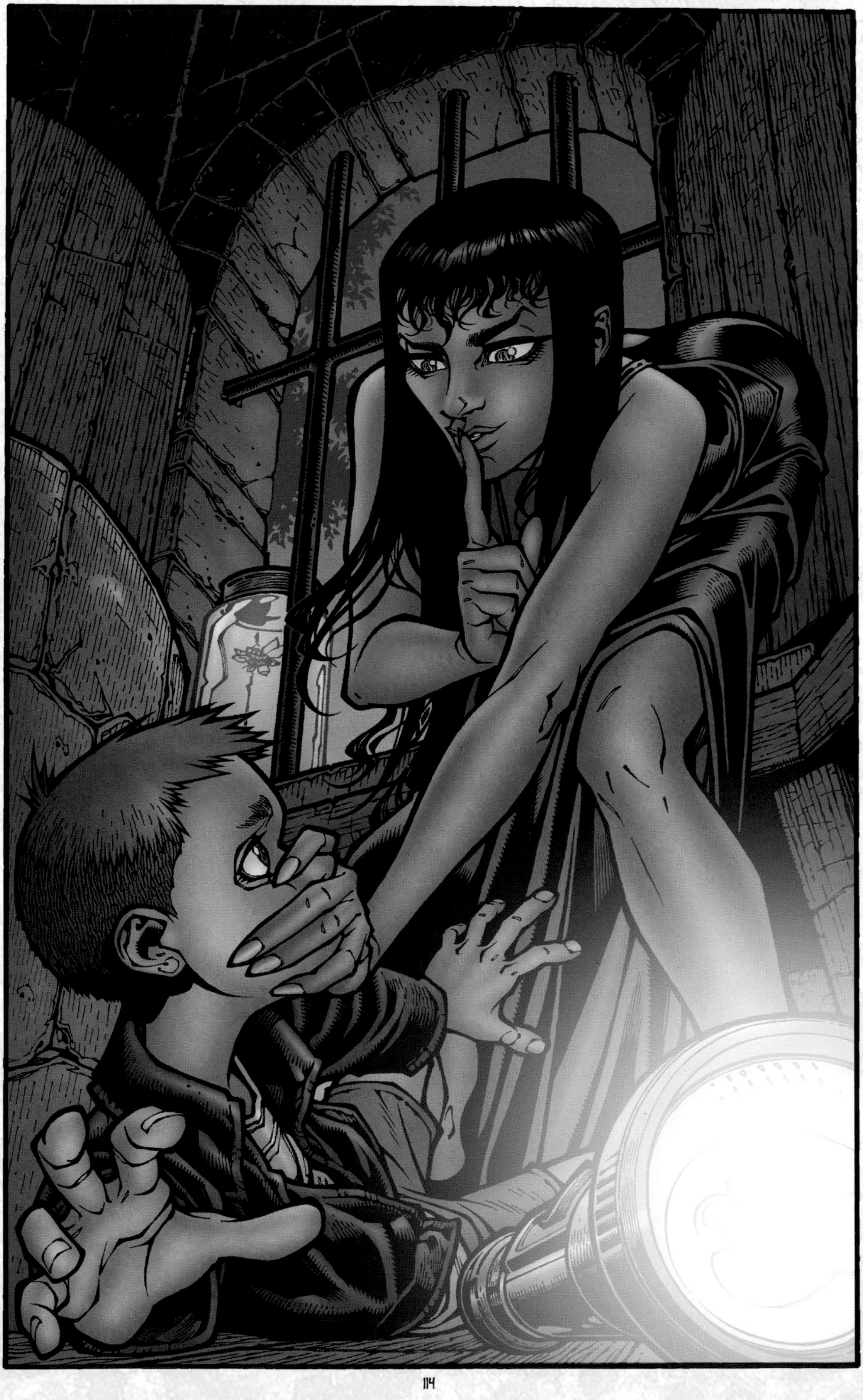

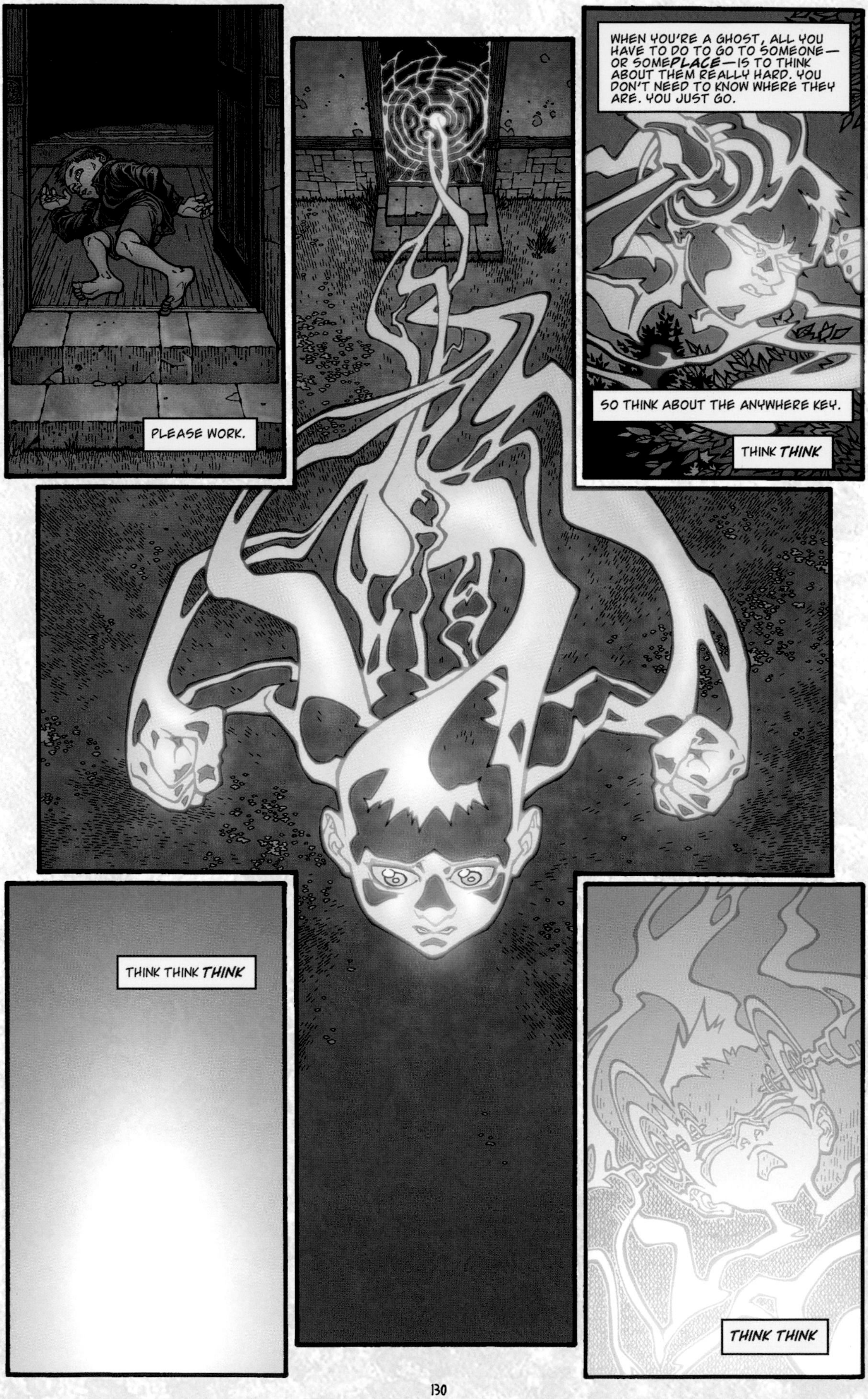
PLEASE WORK.
WHEN YOU'RE A GHOST, ALL YOU HAVE TO DO TO GO TO SOMEONE— OR SOMEPLACE—IS TO THINK ABOUT THEM REALLY HARD. YOU DON'T NEED TO KNOW WHERE THEY ARE. YOU JUST GO.
SO THINK ABOUT THE ANYWHERE KEY.
THINK THINK
THINK THINK THINK
THINK THINK

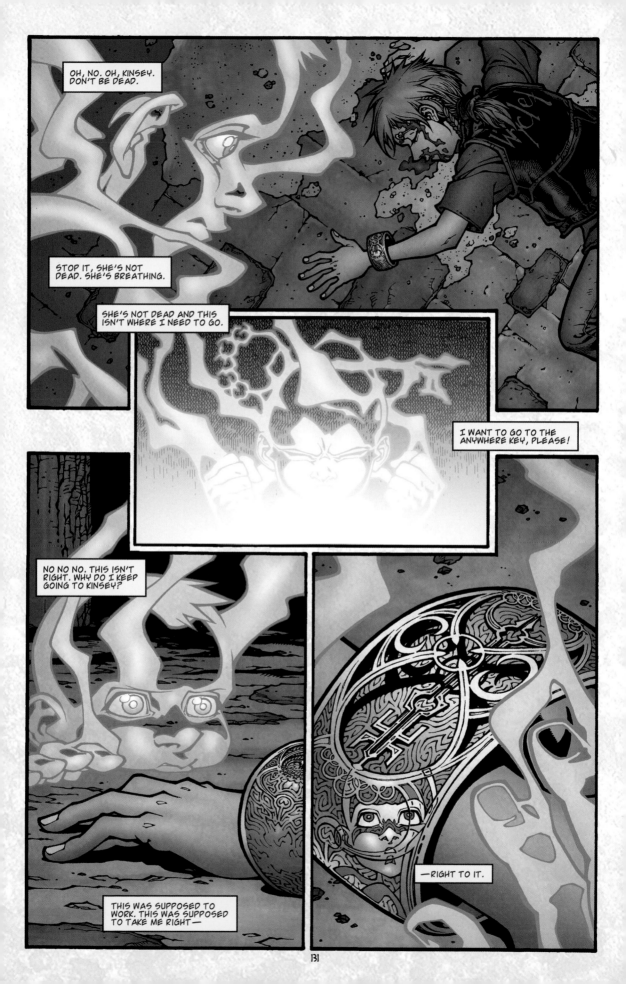

OH, NO. OH, KINSEY. DON'T BE DEAD.

STOP IT, SHE'S NOT DEAD. SHE'S BREATHING.

SHE'S NOT DEAD AND THIS ISN'T WHERE I NEED TO GO.

I WANT TO GO TO THE ANYWHERE KEY, PLEASE!

NO NO NO. THIS ISN'T RIGHT. WHY DO I KEEP GOING TO KINSEY?

THIS WAS SUPPOSED TO WORK. THIS WAS SUPPOSED TO TAKE ME RIGHT—

—RIGHT TO IT.

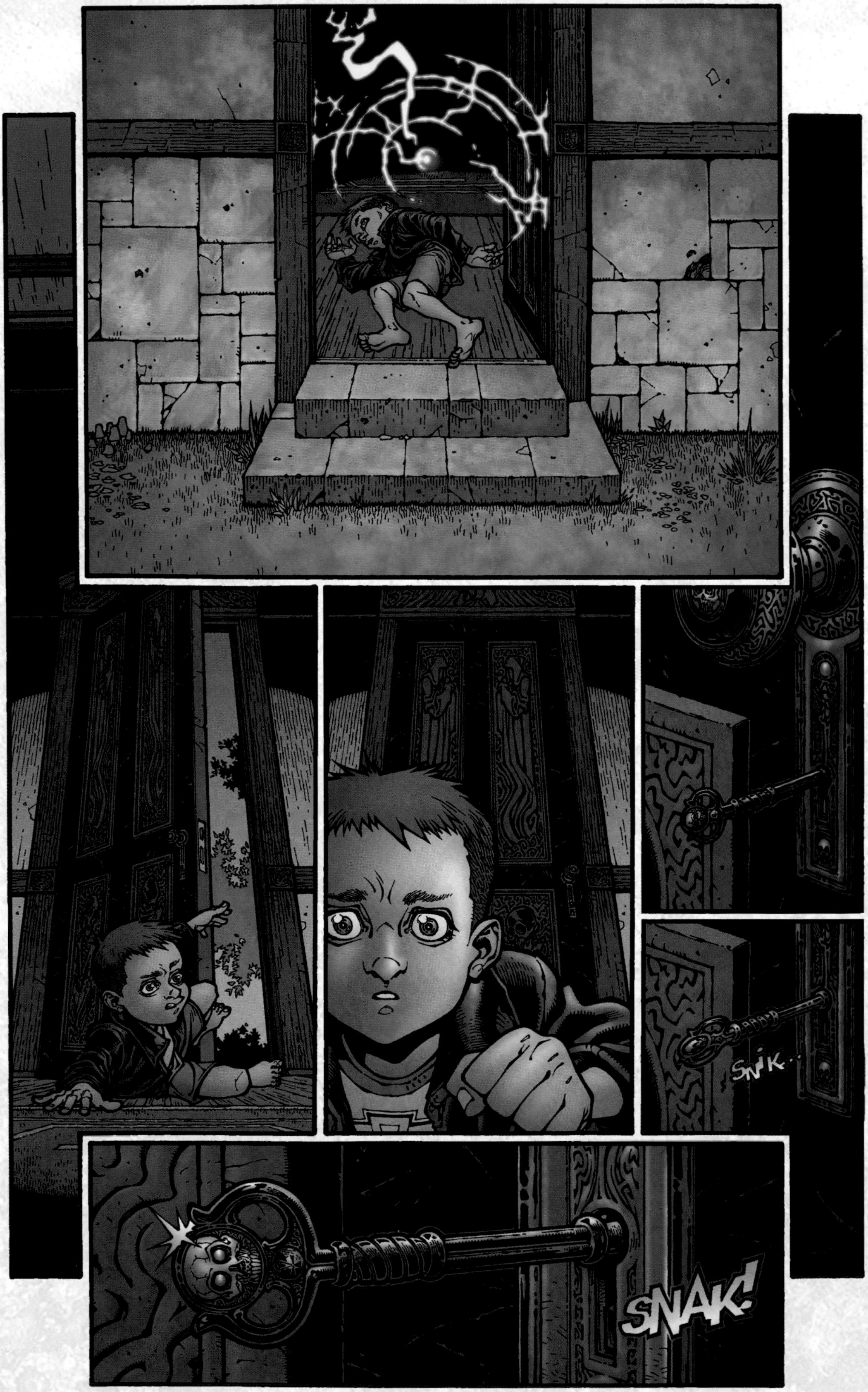

SNIK...
SNAK!

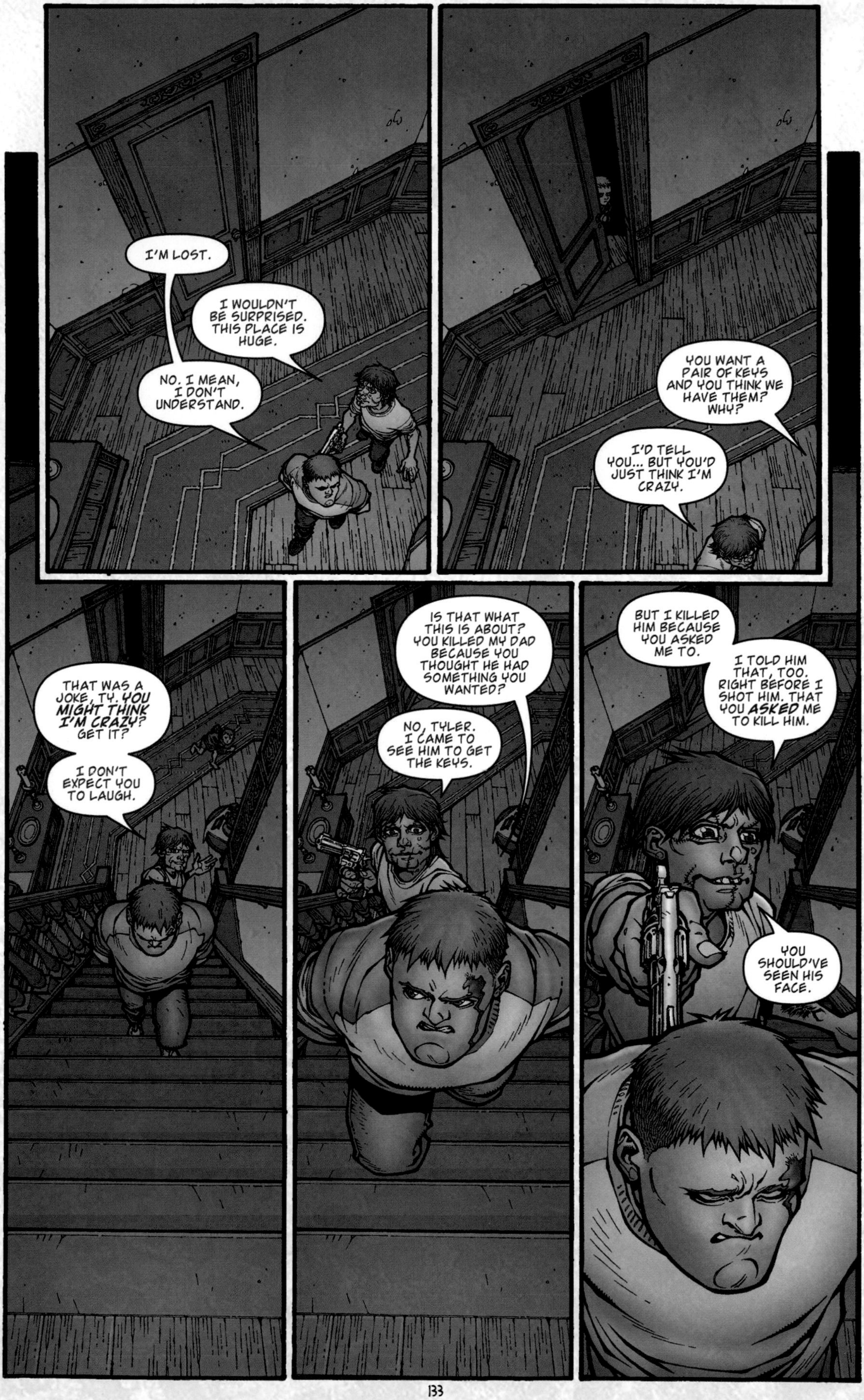
I'M LOST.
I WOULDN'T BE SURPRISED. THIS PLACE IS HUGE.
NO. I MEAN, I DON'T UNDERSTAND.
YOU WANT A PAIR OF KEYS AND YOU THINK WE HAVE THEM? WHY?
I'D TELL YOU... BUT YOU'D JUST THINK I'M CRAZY.
THAT WAS A JOKE, TY. YOU MIGHT THINK I'M CRAZY? GET IT?
I DON'T EXPECT YOU TO LAUGH.
IS THAT WHAT THIS IS ABOUT? YOU KILLED MY DAD BECAUSE YOU THOUGHT HE HAD SOMETHING YOU WANTED?
NO, TYLER. I CAME TO SEE HIM TO GET THE KEYS.
BUT I KILLED HIM BECAUSE YOU ASKED ME TO.
I TOLD HIM THAT, TOO. RIGHT BEFORE I SHOT HIM. THAT YOU ASKED ME TO KILL HIM.
YOU SHOULD'VE SEEN HIS FACE.

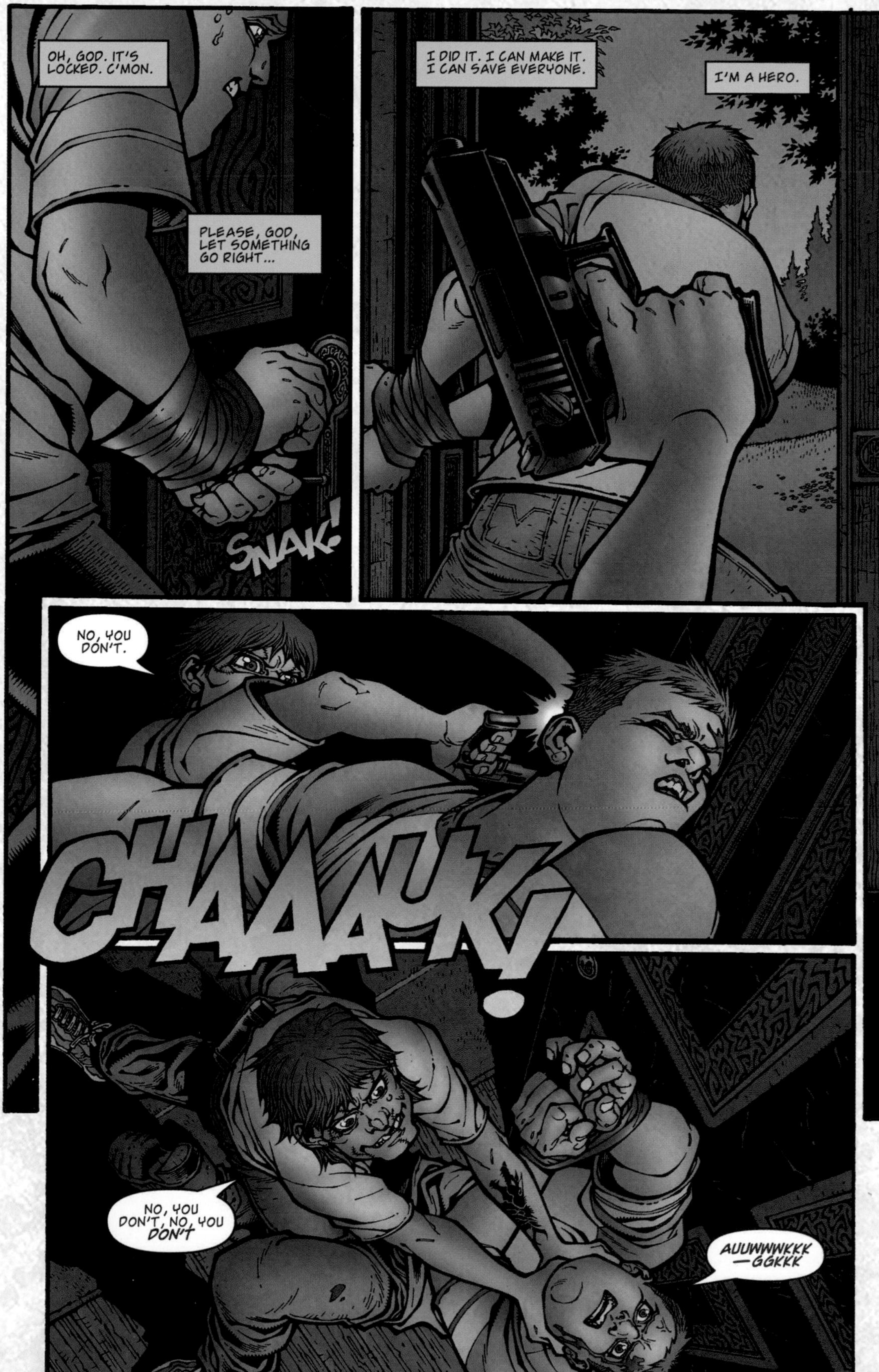

OH, GOD. IT'S LOCKED. C'MON.
PLEASE, GOD, LET SOMETHING GO RIGHT...
SNAK!
I DID IT. I CAN MAKE IT. I CAN SAVE EVERYONE.
I'M A HERO.
NO, YOU DON'T.
CHAAAK!
NO, YOU DON'T, NO, YOU DON'T
AUUWWKKK —GGKKK

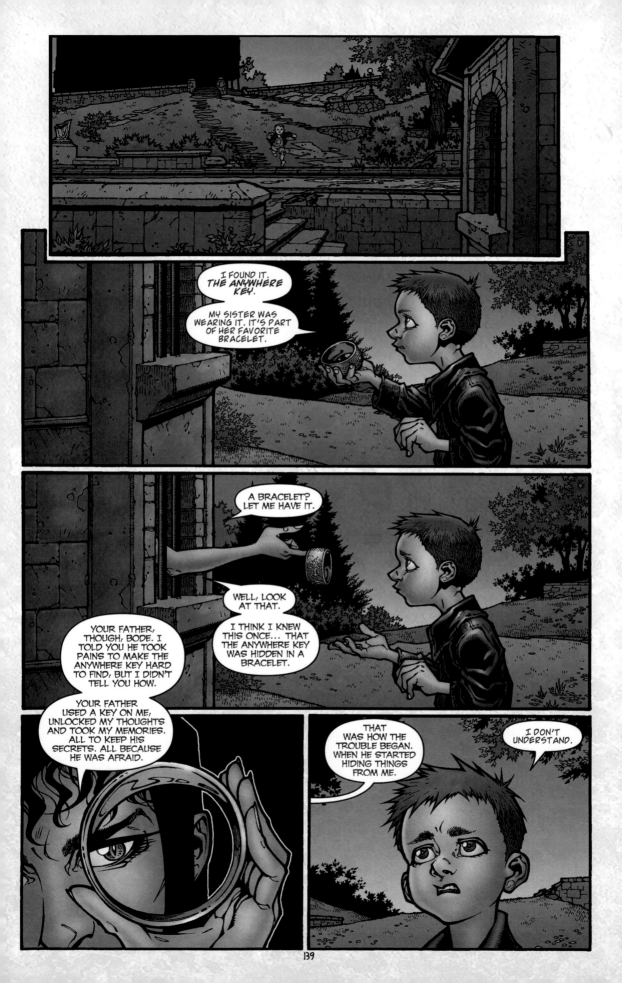

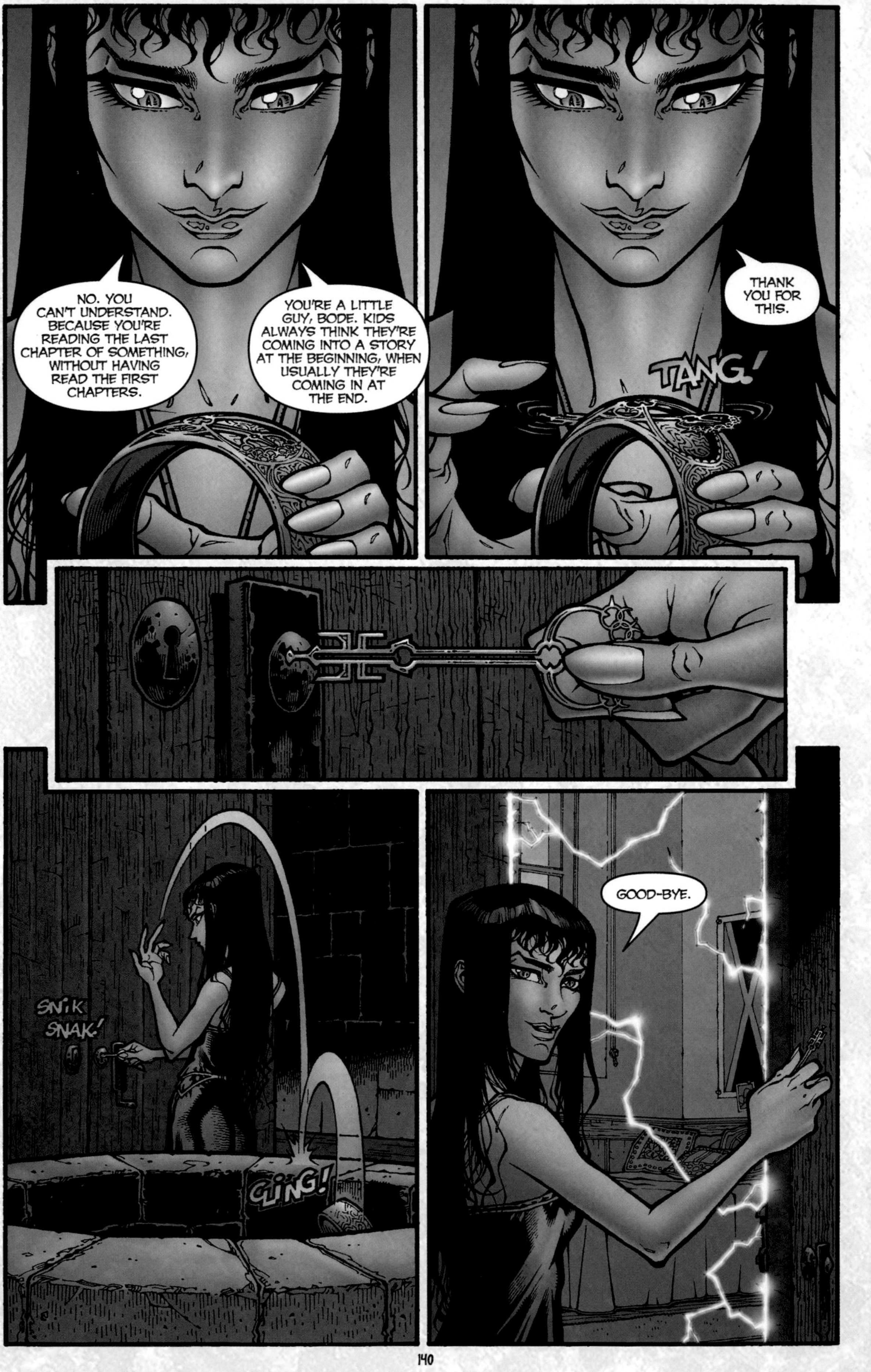
NO. YOU CAN'T UNDERSTAND. BECAUSE YOU'RE READING THE LAST CHAPTER OF SOMETHING, WITHOUT HAVING READ THE FIRST CHAPTERS.
YOU'RE A LITTLE GUY, BODE. KIDS ALWAYS THINK THEY'RE COMING INTO A STORY AT THE BEGINNING, WHEN USUALLY THEY'RE COMING IN AT THE END.
THANK YOU FOR THIS.
TANG!
SNIK SNAK!
CLING!
GOOD-BYE.

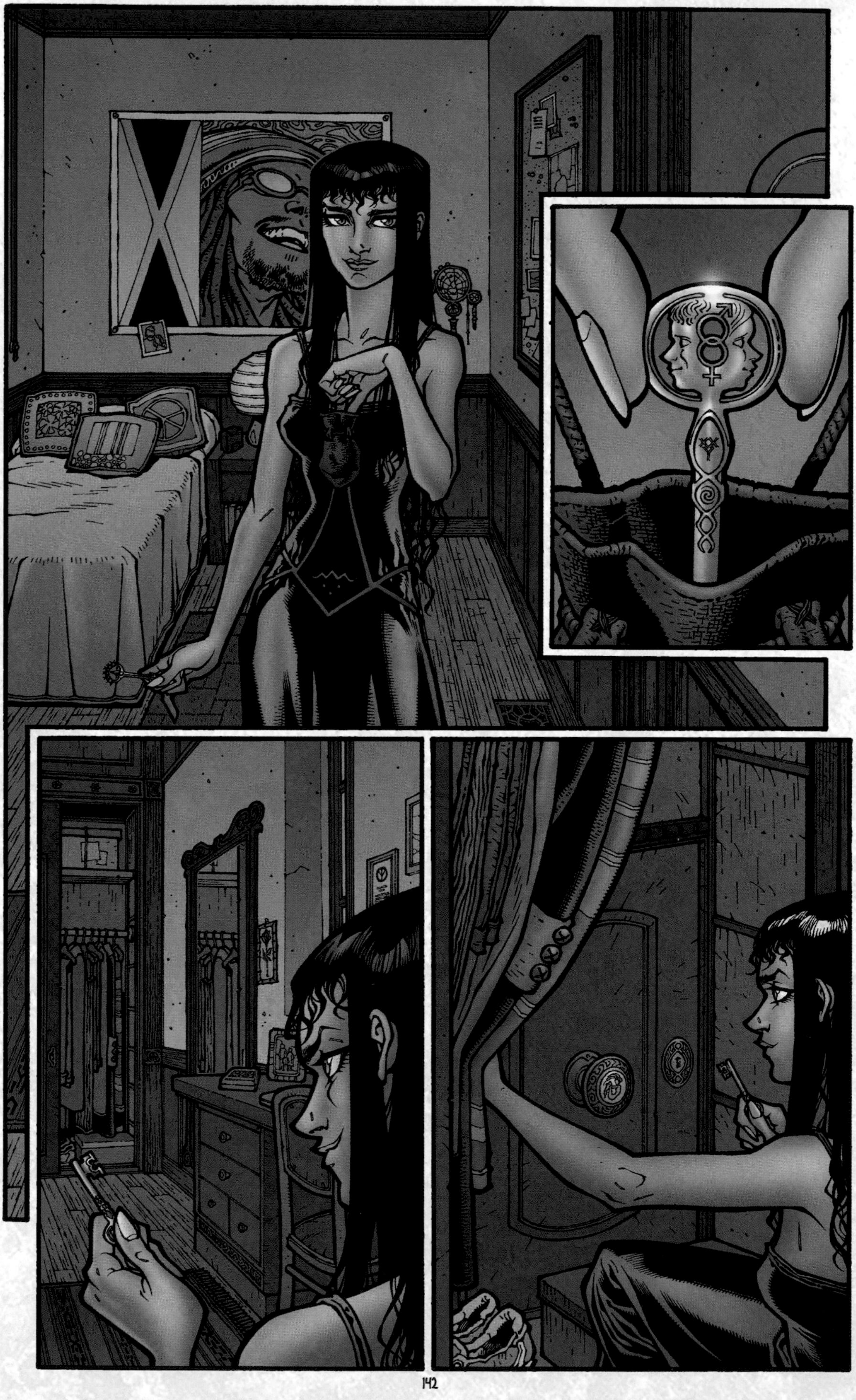

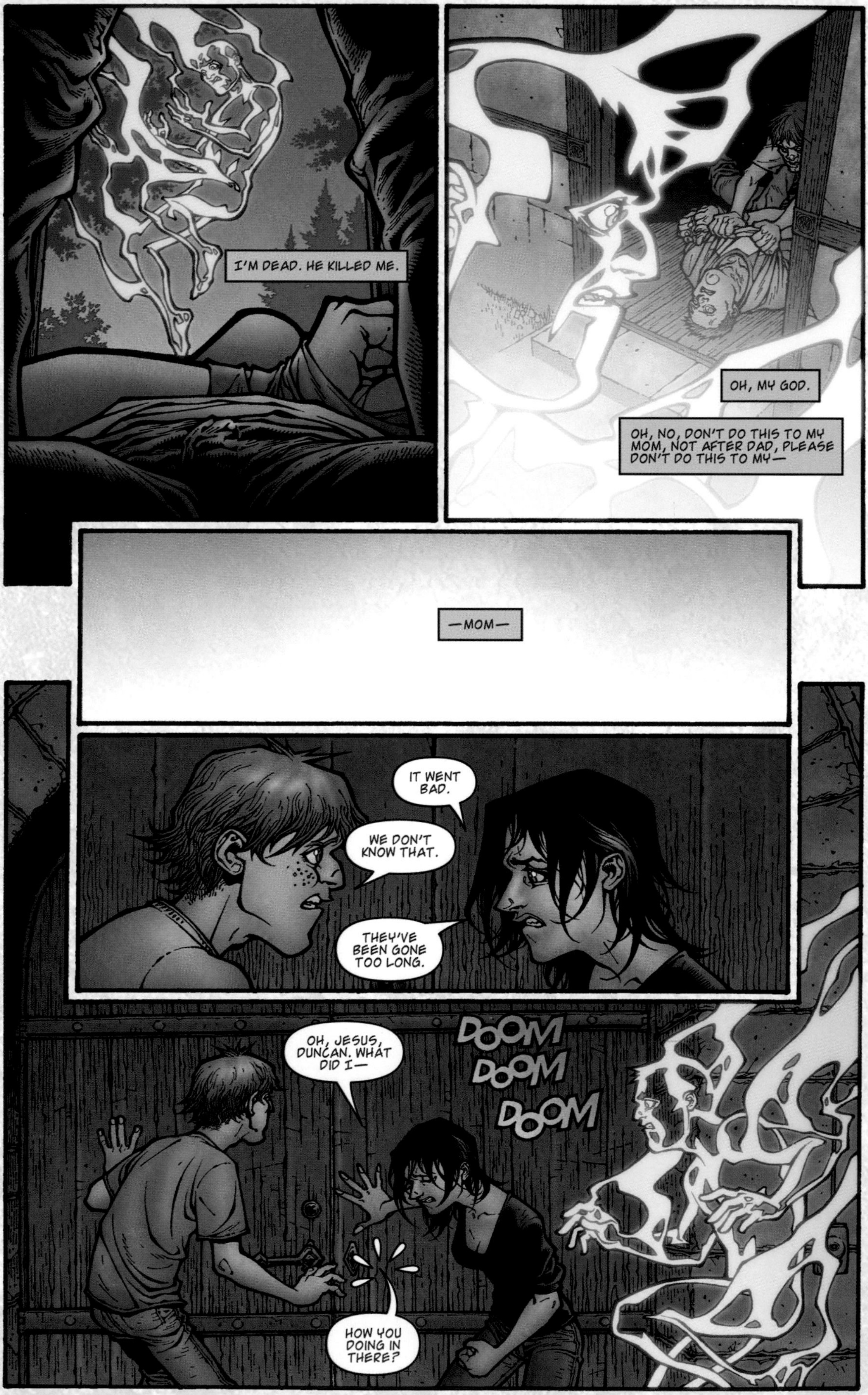
I'M DEAD. HE KILLED ME.
OH, MY GOD.
OH, NO, DON'T DO THIS TO MY MOM, NOT AFTER DAD, PLEASE DON'T DO THIS TO MY—
—MOM—
IT WENT BAD.
WE DON'T KNOW THAT.
THEY'VE BEEN GONE TOO LONG.
OH, JESUS, DUNCAN. WHAT DID I—
DOOM DOOM DOOM
HOW YOU DOING IN THERE?

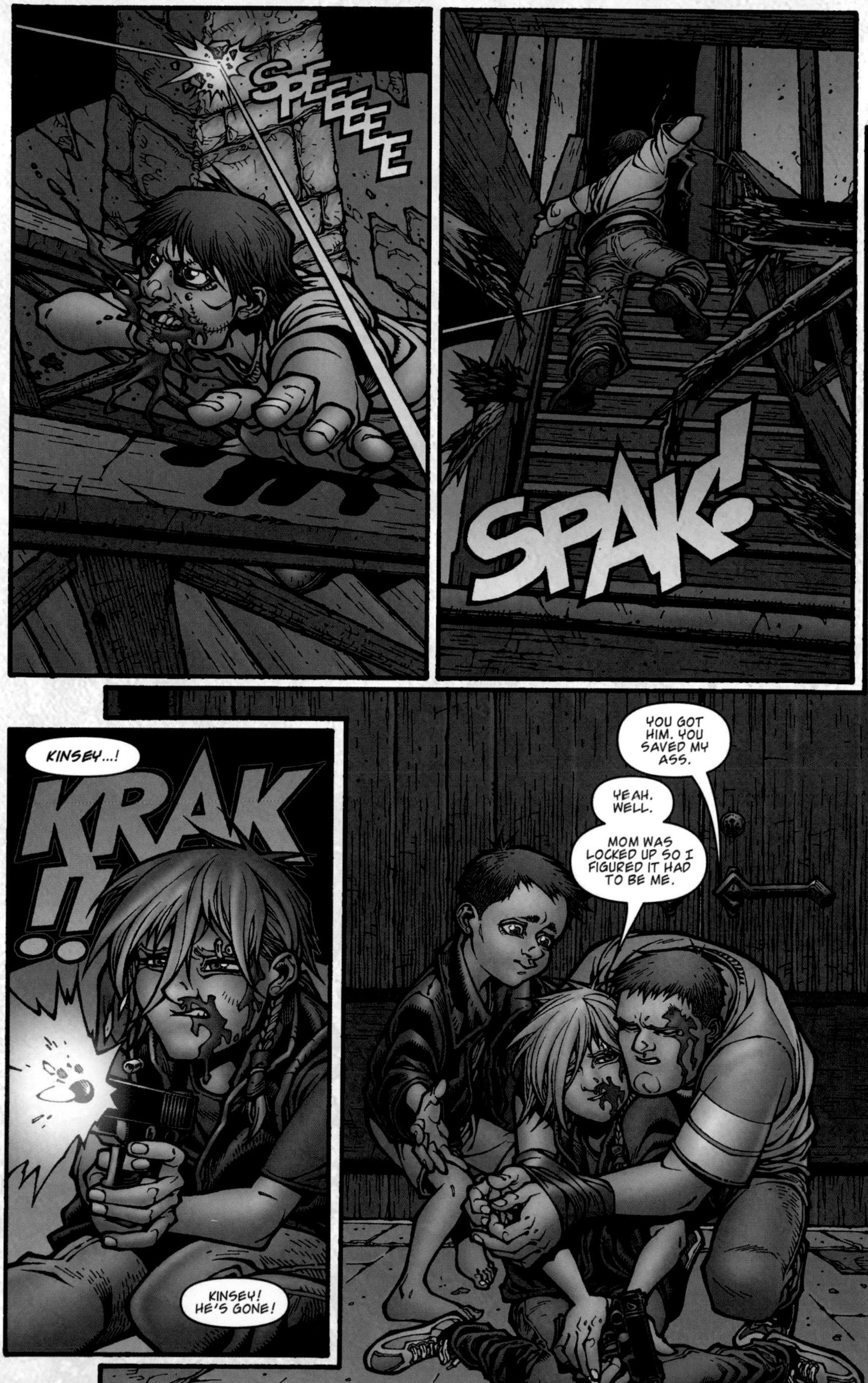
SPEEEEEE
SPAK!
KINSEY...!
KRAK!!
KINSEY! HE'S GONE!
YOU GOT HIM. YOU SAVED MY ASS.
YEAH. WELL.
MOM WAS LOCKED UP SO I FIGURED IT HAD TO BE ME.

CHONG
CHONG
CHONG

CHONG
CHONG

CHONG

OH, COME ON.

GODDAM PRANK, IF THIS IS ONE OF MY KIDS, GODDAM BETTER BE READY TO RUN THEIR BEST.

COMING!

HEY, YOU CLOWNS. IF THIS IS A JOKE AND MY BOY GETS WOKE UP, THE PUNCH LINE IS GOING TO BE ONE PISSED OFF COACH MAKING A PACK OF SNOTNOSE KIDS RUN SUICIDES ALL—

HELLO, ELLIE. YOU LOOK GREAT. MIND IF I COME IN?

I MEAN, I KILLED YOUR MOTHER FOR YOU. IT'S REALLY THE LEAST YOU CAN DO.

TCHICK

I'D LIKE ANOTHER LOOK AT WHERE SAM WOUND UP.

SURE, NO PROBLEM. LET ME UNLOCK—

WAIT, WHAT ARE YOU—

I SUPPOSE HE WAS TRYING TO GET OUTSIDE. MAYBE DRAG HIS WAY BACK TO THE BOAT.

BUT THEN... HM.

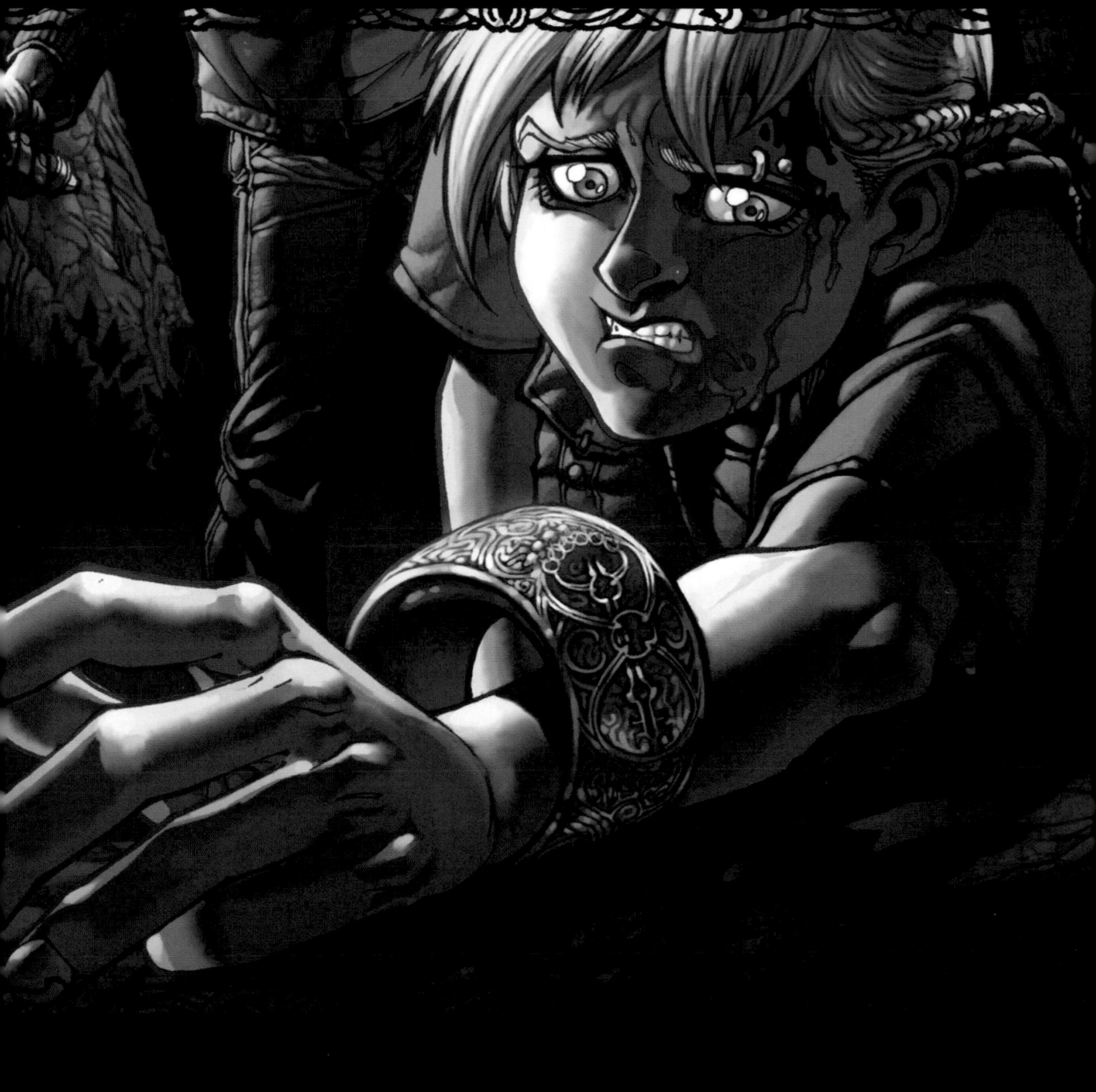

ART GALLERY

BY GABRIEL RODRIGUEZ

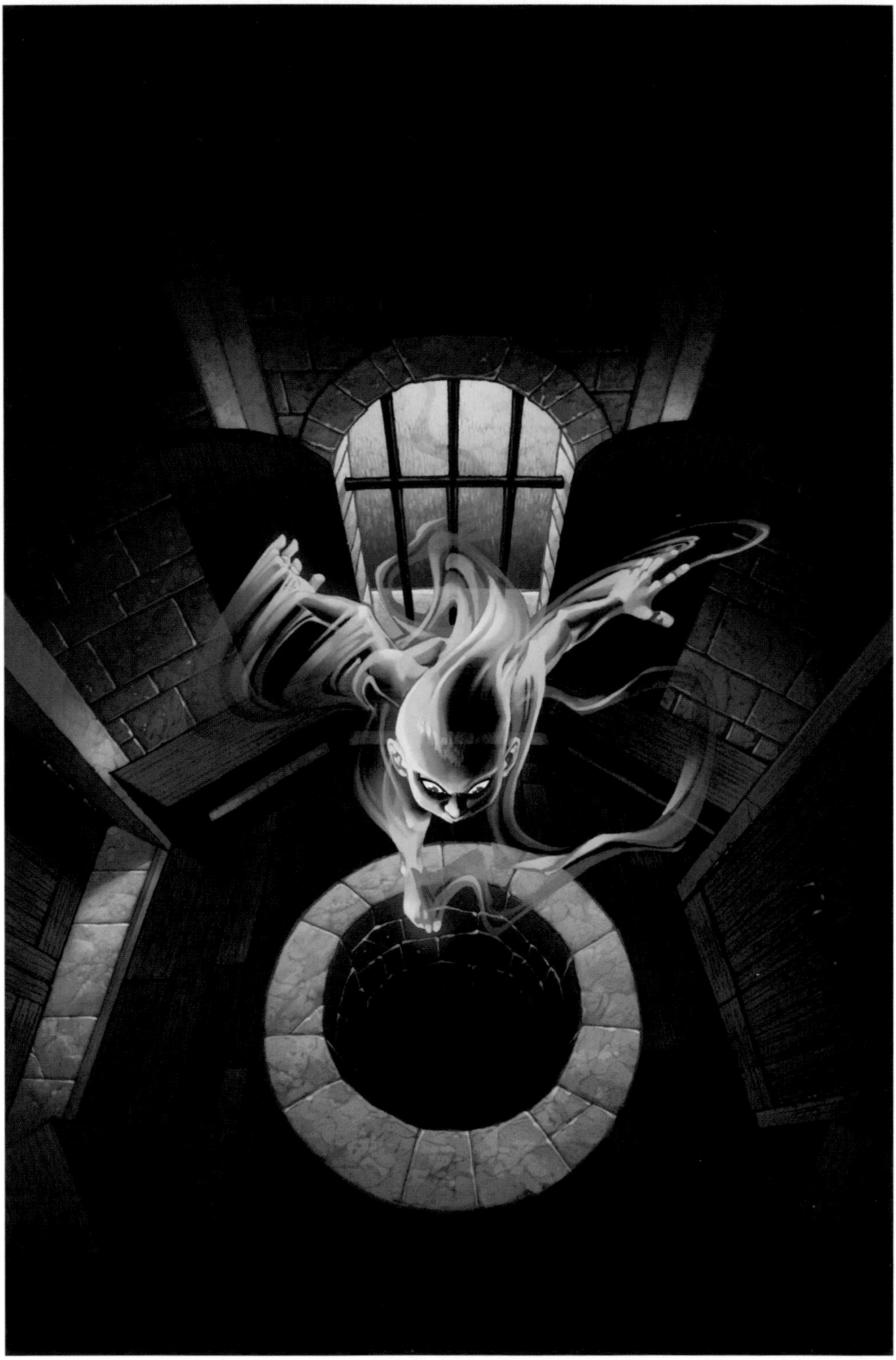

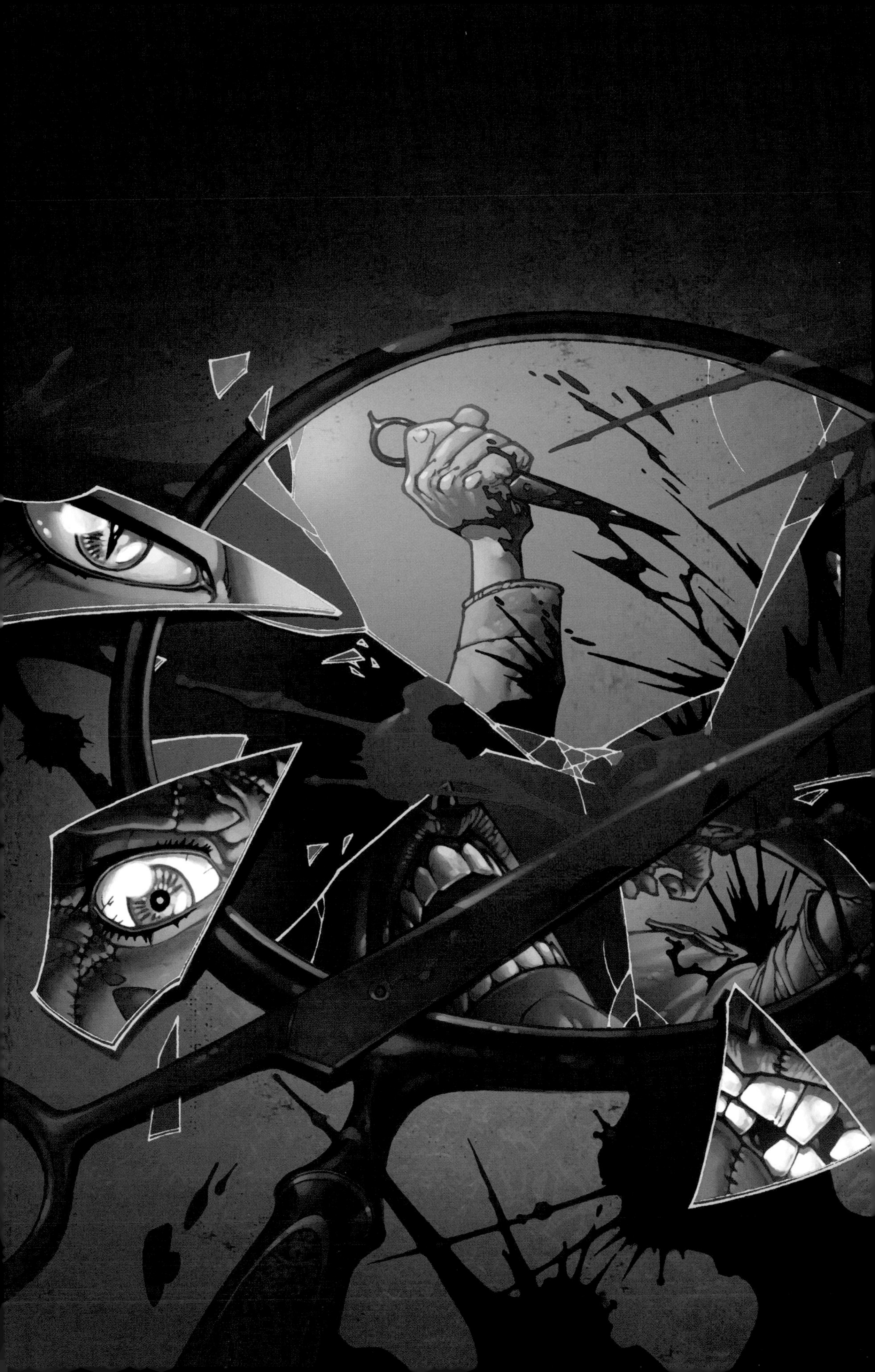

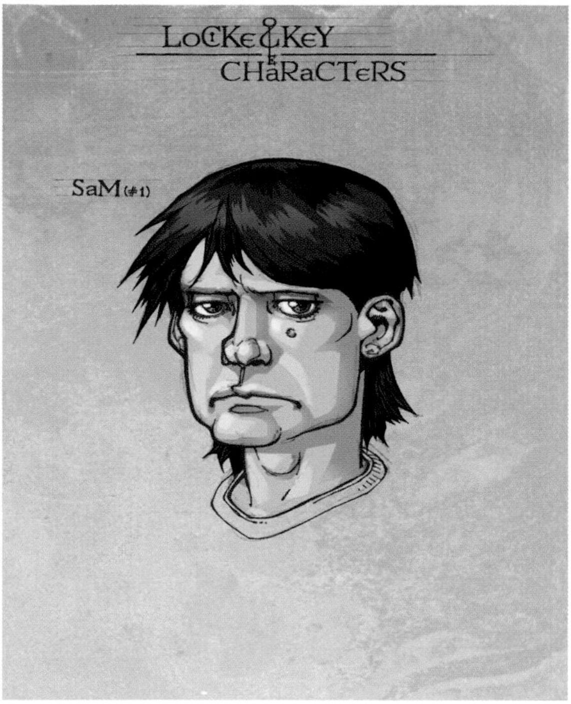
LoCKe & KeY
CHaRaCTeRS
SaM (#1)

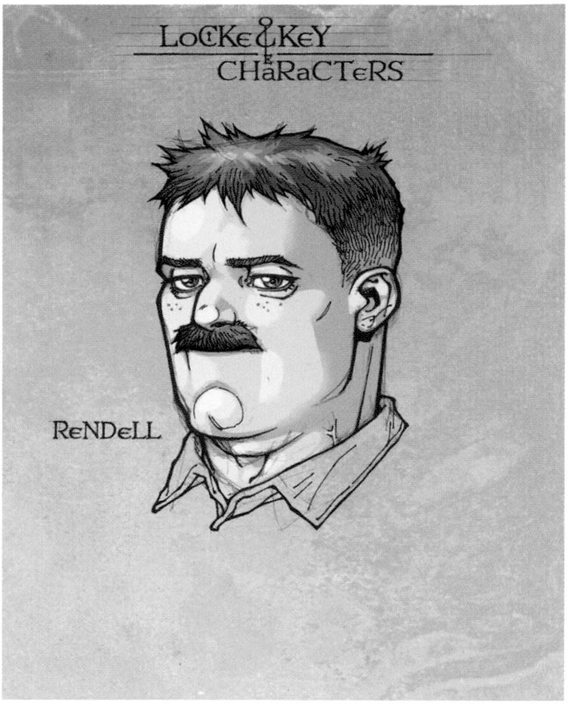
LoCKe & KeY
CHaRaCTeRS
ReNDeLL

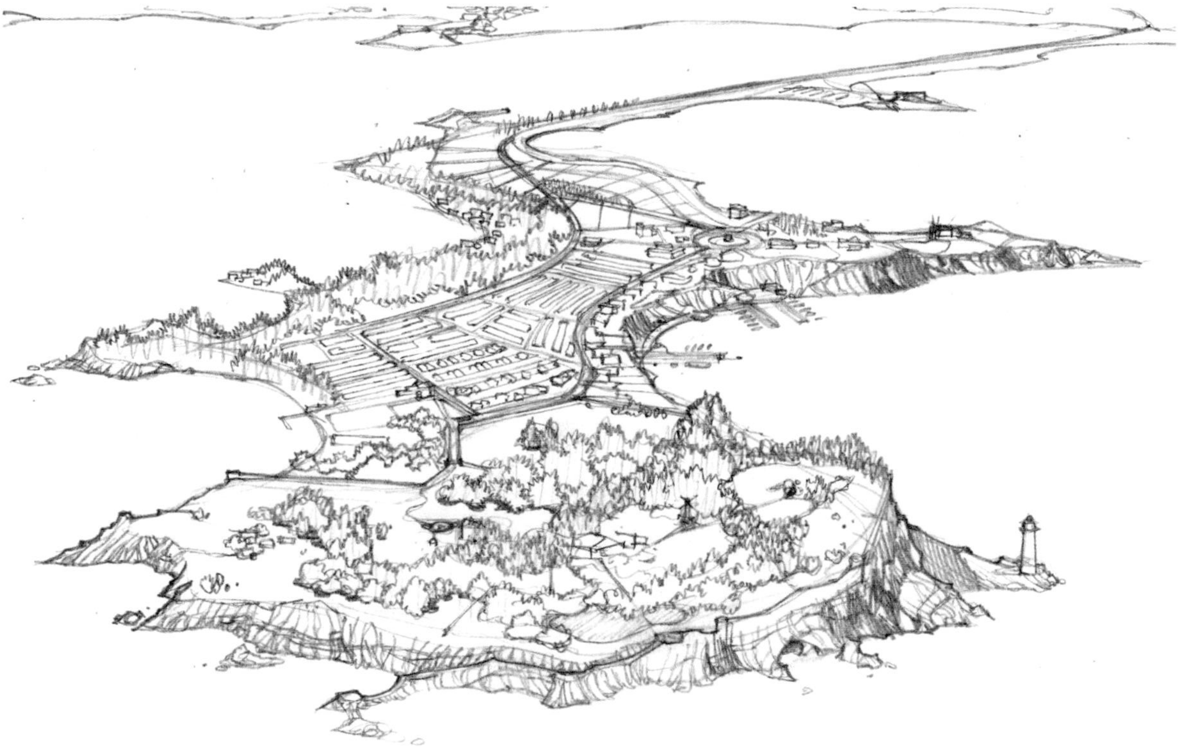

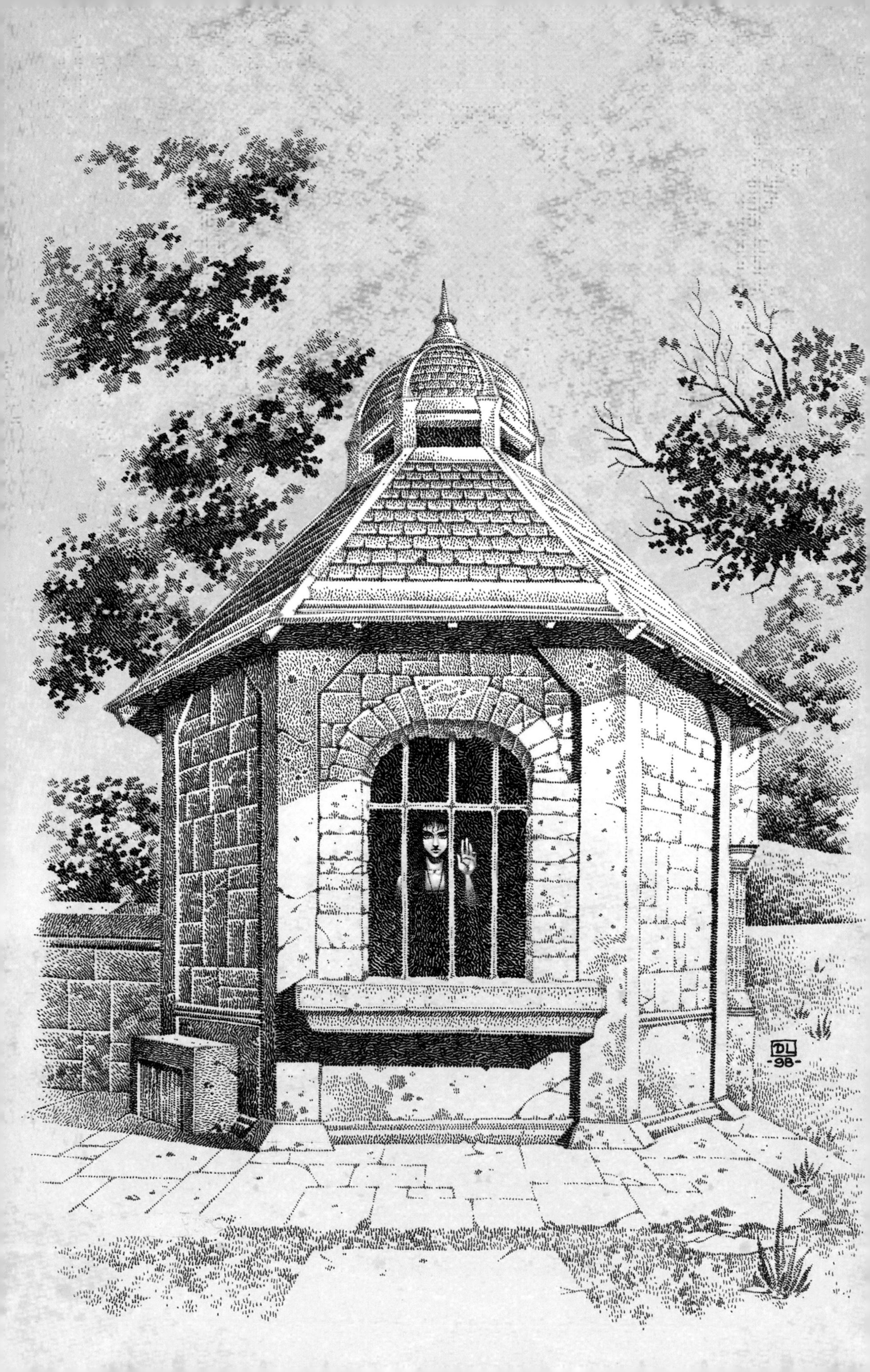

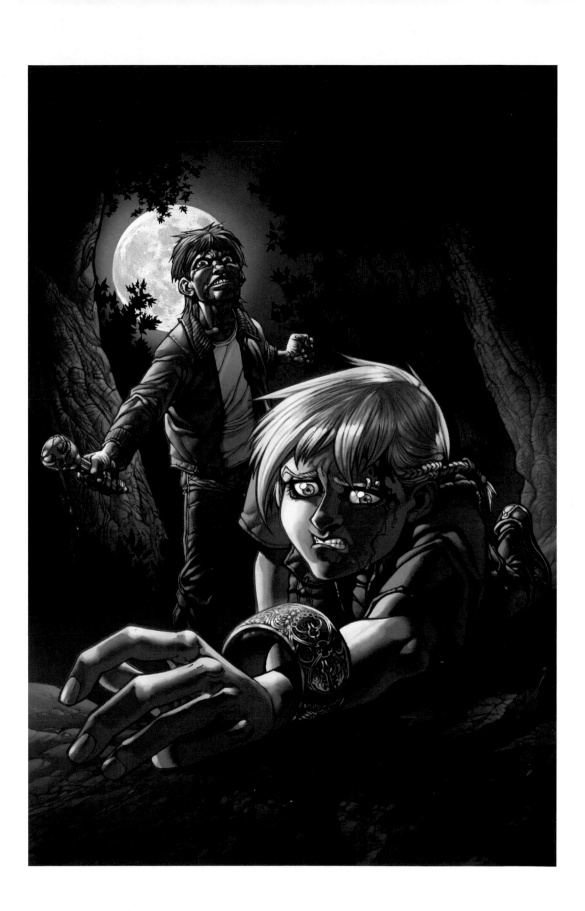

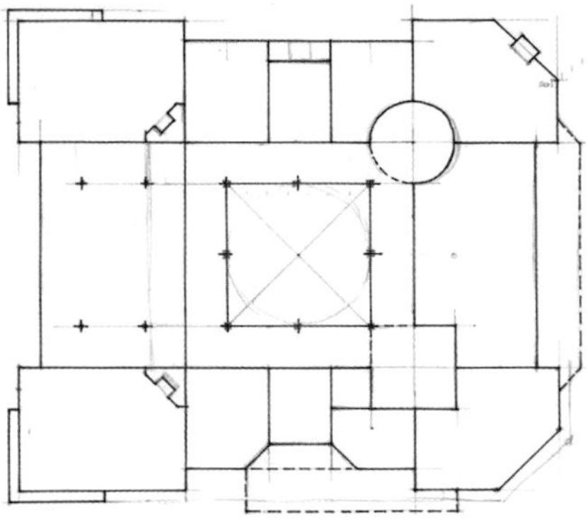
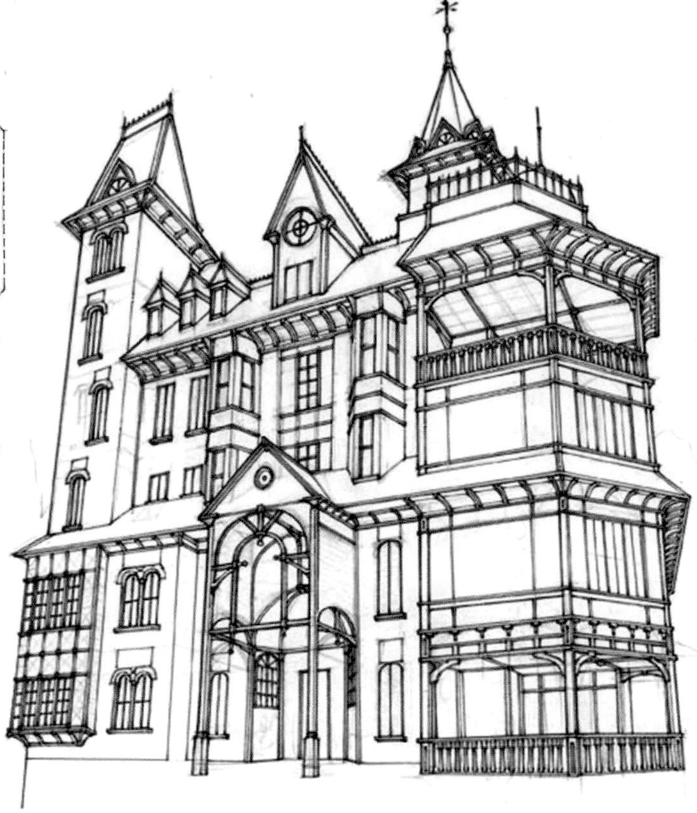
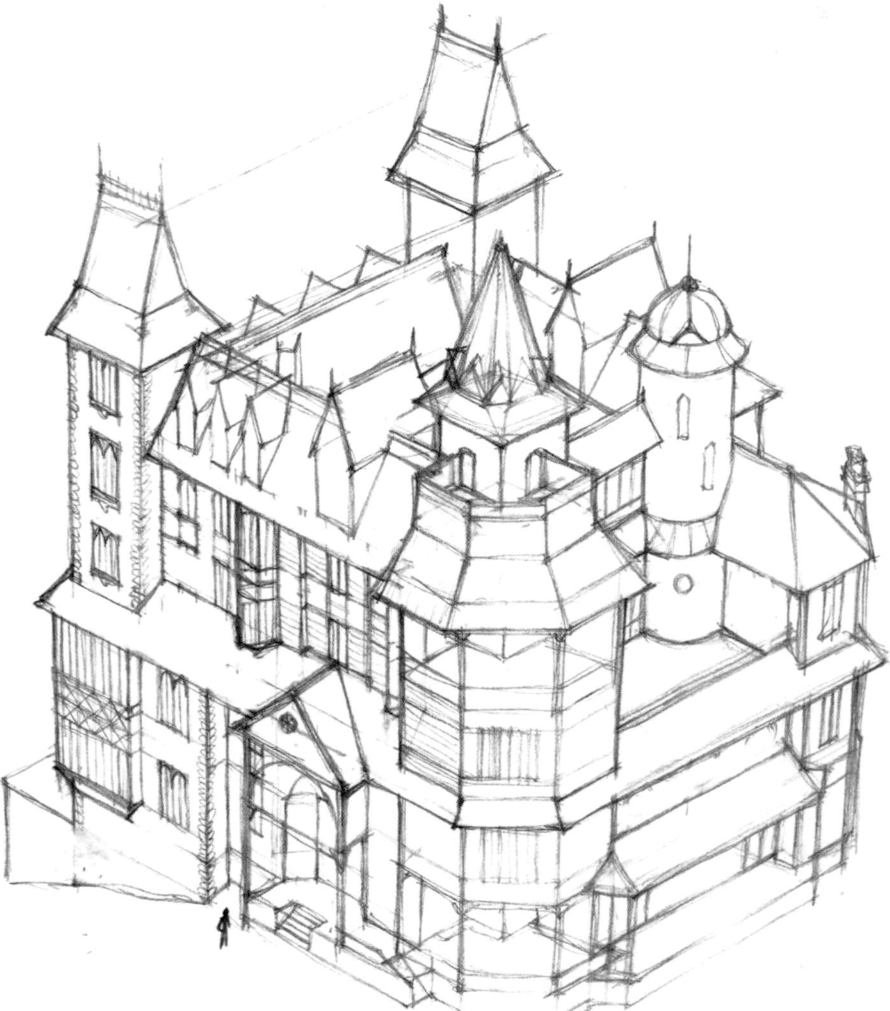

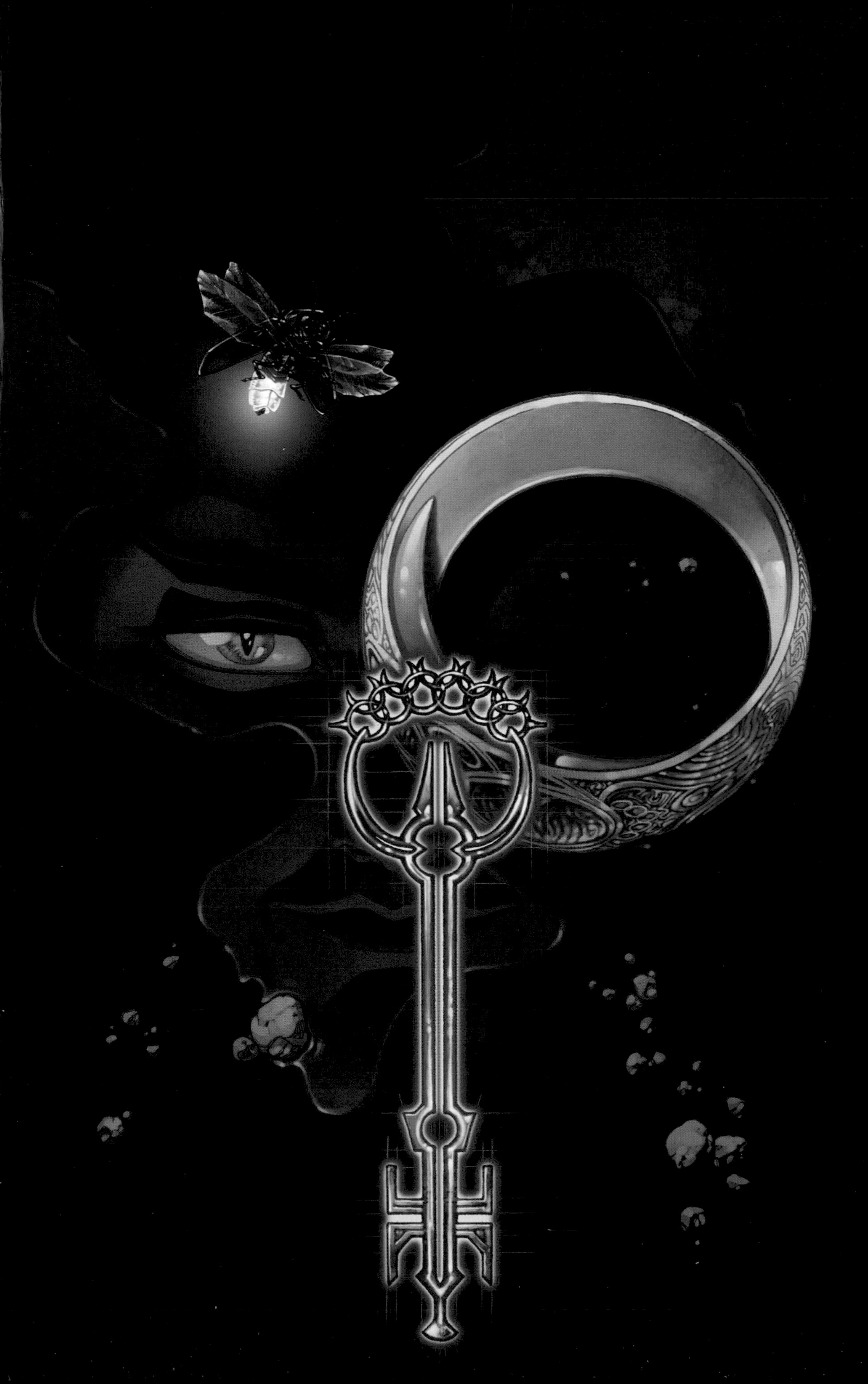

Joe Hill is the author of a novel, *Heart-Shaped Box*, and a collection of stories, *20th Century Ghosts*. He is currently at work on a new novel, *The Surrealist's Glass*. The worst comic book he ever read was still a pretty good time. He has a Web site, joehillfiction.com, where you can find out stuff.

Gabriel Rodriguez is a supremely gifted Chilean artist and co-creator of the twisted but wonderful world of *Locke & Key*. The invitation to participate in the fantastic journey of the surviving members of the Locke family, conceived by Joe Hill, has become a dream project made real for Gabriel. He asks that readers unlock their hearts and minds, and accept an invitation into new realms and tales, thrilling experiences, and secret places that his efforts craft into a vivid universe.

In addition to his current work in *Locke & Key*, Gabriel has collaborated with IDW on *Clive Barker's The Great And Secret Show*, *Beowulf*, and *George A. Romero's Land of the Dead*, as well as several *CSI* comics.

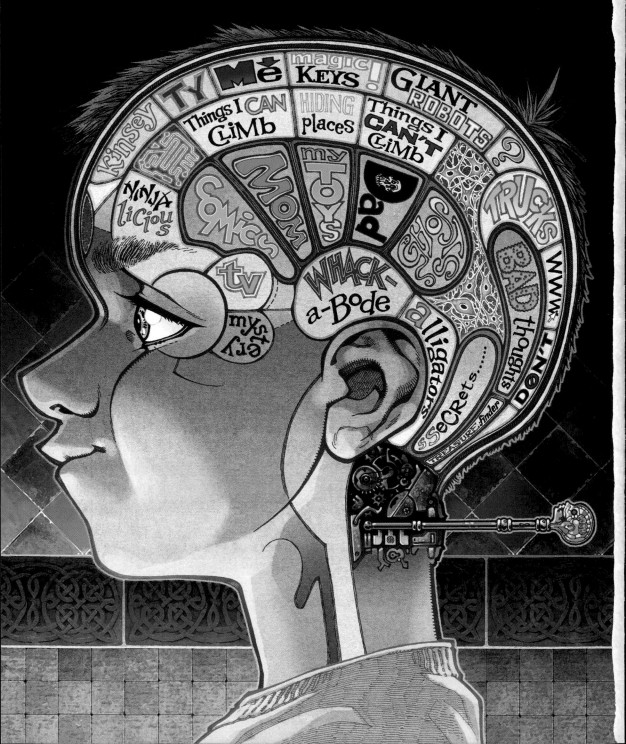